# Hispanic
## Albuquerque

The statue in Old Town
of Governor Francisco
Cuervo y Valdés, founder
of Albuquerque.
(Photograph courtesy
of Michelle Holtby)

# Hispanic Albuquerque

## 1706–1846

MARC SIMMONS

University of New Mexico Press

Albuquerque

Library of Congress Cataloging-in-Publication Data

Simmons, Marc.
    Hispanic Albuquerque, 1706–1846 / Marc Simmons.
        p.   cm.
Includes bibliographical references (p.    ) and index.
    ISBN 0-8263-3160-2 (pbk. : alk. paper)
    1. Hispanic Americans—New Mexico—Albuquerque—History—
18th century.   2. Hispanic Americans—New Mexico—Albuquerque—
History—19th century.   3. Albuquerque (N.M.)—History—18th
century.   4. Albuquerque (N.M.)—History—19th century.
5. Albuquerque (N.M.)—Ethnic relations.   6. Indians of North
America—New Mexico—Albuquerque—History—18th century.
7. Indians of North America—New Mexico—Albuquerque—History—
19th century.   8. Indians, Treatment of—New Mexico—Albuquerque—
History.   9. Frontier and pioneer life—New Mexico—Albuquerque.
I. Title.

F804.A3 S56 2003
978.9'6102—dc21

                            2002154495

The research for the unabridged edition was made possible by a grant
from the National Endowment for the Humanities.

Design by Melissa Tandysh

*Para*
*Conchita Lucero*
*y*
*Millie Santillanes*

# Contents

# Preface

SOCIAL OBSERVER V. B. PRICE has referred to Albuquerque as "an eccentric city," by which is meant one that has managed, against heavy odds, to maintain some measure of individuality. Of the many different threads braiding together that go into shaping Albuquerque's distinctive personality, the city's Hispanic heritage must be rated as one of the more enduring and significant.

Three centuries ago, in the spring of 1706, Spanish Governor Francisco Cuervo y Valdés provided for the founding of the new Villa of Albuquerque. It was located in New Mexico's Middle Rio Grande Valley within the Province of Tiguex, home to a cluster of a dozen or more Tiwa-speaking Indian pueblos.

The history of the community's growth during the following 115 years of the Spanish colonial period, and its struggles to adapt to swift changes that began in the

25-year interval 1821 to 1846, when an independent Mexico governed New Mexico, forms the subject of this volume. The fate of Hispanic Albuquerqueans under American rule, extending from the formation of a New Mexico territorial government in 1850 down to the present, is left to another book.

This narrative also gives attention to the life ways and cultural traditions of Albuquerque citizens during the eighteenth and early nineteenth centuries. It is plain that these Spanish pioneers were a tough and spirited people, able to rely upon their own resources, ingenuity, and capacity to endure. At times they could, moreover, be contentious as court records and government documents vividly reveal.

One small but confusing matter should be clarified at the outset. The city took its name from the Duke of Alburquerque, Viceroy of New Spain, who spelled that name with an extra *r*. Spanish and Mexican documents continued to use the traditional spelling as late as the 1840s. But then, with the coming of the Anglo-Americans, whose tongues tripped over the long and unfamiliar word, the first *r* fell away and *Alburquerque* became *Albuquerque*. For the sake of consistency, I have employed the latter form throughout, except in those cases when reference is made directly to the Duke.

The contents of *Hispanic Albuquerque* first appeared in 1982 as the opening chapters in my comprehensive volume, *Albuquerque: A Narrative History*. That work has long been out of print and thus not readily accessible to the public. Since the present offering is intended for the general reader, the usual scholarly appendages that appeared in the original—endnotes and bibliography—have been omitted. For convenient reference, however, a list of suggested readings has been added at the end.

Of the many ills associated with our heavy-handed modernity, the loss of a sense of history is one of the more damaging. Serious study of the past instructs, inspires, and entertains. Without it—without memory of what went before us—we are forced to skate on the surface of life, now largely shaped and trivialized by the commodification of almost everything.

In probing the early record of Albuquerque, during the years prior to 1850, the author found a dramatic, engaging, even exotic story. In the telling, it is hoped that readers will encounter some of the enchantment and mystery that readily excites the historical imagination and that will encourage further study of this and other worlds that are now gone.

Marc Simmons
Cerrillos, New Mexico
September 2002

One of the earliest and most valuable lessons history teaches to such as can be taught anything is that you and I and our times are not the earth and the fullness thereof, but mere drops in an inevitable tide. Incredible as it may seem, there was some world before we got here. And when we can face and begin to grasp that inconsiderate truth, we are in a fair way to be able to get some good out of history.

—*Charles F. Lummis*

# 1

## *Introduction*

THE COMING OF CORONADO and his brash cavaliers to Puebloland marked a watershed in the long history of New Mexico's Indian people. After centuries of comparative isolation, they were now to be drawn into close and irritating contact with Europeans, whose alien ways and beliefs would upset the old familiar pattern of native life, the roots of which traced back to the Desert Culture of the pre-Christian era. Thus, the year 1540 was a turning point for the Indians. And it was also a benchmark in the story of Albuquerque, for the claiming and initial exploration of New Mexico set in motion the sequence of events that provide the background for the city's founding.

What kind of men were these who followed Francisco Vásquez de Coronado a thousand miles northward from Mexico into unknown lands seeking adventure and mythical kingdoms filled with treasure? In answering that question, we come a long way toward understanding the mentality and motives of those Spaniards who later became the founders and builders of the Province of New Mexico.

The Spanish conquistador of the sixteenth century was a restless, undisciplined, prideful, courageous bundle of energy with strict loyalties to his king and his religion, and with a consuming ambition for wealth and social status. His appetite for life and enthusiasm for adventure led him across the greater portion of two continents, making possible seemingly impossible conquests. The hereditary poverty and austere customs of his native Spain ably fitted him to endure without complaint the severe hardships met in the New World. Whether through an inborn sense of fatalism or a simple lack of foresight, the fact is, he was prone to improvidence, to impatience with long-range planning. As a man of action, he wanted immediate results. For him, the monotony of daily toil held no interest.

In spite of a poor showing in his treatment of the Indians, especially in the early years, the Spaniard at heart believed the native people possessed certain natural rights guaranteeing protection of their lives and property. But herein lay seeds of trouble: the conquistadores, along with the civil governors and missionaries who succeeded them, were also convinced that as chosen servants of God and the Spanish king, it fell to them to define and administer such rights and at the same time to reshape the Indian, for his own good, in the image prescribed by Hispanic Catholicism. These conceited and inflexible notions often bore bitter fruit, and nowhere was that harvest more unsweet than in New Mexico.

Coronado's knights, who, with Hernando de Alvarado, made first contact with the Tiwa pueblos, were by all accounts a bantam-sized lot, averaging probably under 5.5 feet in height, as did most Europeans of the day. Life's grinding hardships coupled with a meager and poorly balanced diet kept man physically small, but that did not prevent him from becoming tough and sinewy. To the Indians, themselves small in stature, the bearded Spaniards dressed in partial body armor, wearing helmets, and carrying harquebuses, crossbows, and swords must have appeared larger than life. As they would soon learn, these strangers were extraordinary men with extraordinary dreams. But at the same time, they were people accustomed to having their way, and woe to anyone who obstructed their path.

Coronado's expedition to discover and explore the mysterious realms of the far north had been organized with much fanfare in central Mexico. To his colors had come scores of young, footloose, rough-and-tumble Spaniards eager for the riches they felt certain abounded among the unknown tribes at the interior of the continent. Fernando Cortés, a mere twenty years before, had found and conquered the glittering Aztec empire, so it seemed entirely plausible that another El Dorado waited in the wilderness for those plucky enough to search it out.

Viceroy Don Antonio de Mendoza, chief representative of the king and the highest civil official in Spanish North America, journeyed amid much pomp and pageantry to the village of Compostela in western Mexico, the launching point for Coronado's grand project. Mendoza desired to bestow his personal blessing upon the undertaking, which he hoped would both expand and enrich the enormous Viceroyalty of New Spain over which he governed. But he, along with

Coronado and the reckless army of adventurers, were all destined for supreme disappointment. New Mexico and the wide lands beyond were to prove barren of treasure.

The Spaniards' frustration and disenchantment help explain, but fail to justify, the treatment accorded the Indians dwelling along the Rio Grande. After the vanguard of the expedition reached the river and received its cordial welcome, Alvarado had hurried a messenger back to his commander, who remained in Zuñi, suggesting the Province of Tiguex as a suitable place to spend the winter.

Coronado accepted the recommendation and put his force in motion toward the Rio Grande. The bloom was off his enthusiasm, for after a punishing march across the deserts and mountains of southern Arizona, the rock and mud pueblos of the Zuñis had yielded no gold. Nor had a brief excursion by one of his lieutenants to the nearby Hopi villages produced anything of value. It had begun to appear that the fabled wealth of the north was pure myth. Yet, it was still too early in the game to give up altogether. With pennants flying and helmet plumes dancing in the breeze, he took up Alvarado's trail for Tiguex on the fond hope that there some faint success might be salvaged.

On the Rio Grande, the first units of the army of three hundred Spaniards made camp close by the walls of the Tiwa town, Alcanfor, believed to be the place we now know as Kuaua. Their tent quarters provided adequate protection while the bracing autumn weather held, but late in the season stiff, chill winds began to creep around the upper end of the Sandia Mountains promising a rigorous winter ahead. As the cold deepened and set teeth to rattling, the distress of the soldiers grew. Their light clothes that served them well in the tropics offered meager defense against New Mexico's icy blasts.

The Indians of Alcanfor were asked to vacate their pueblo so that the Spaniards could move in. They did so without resistance, but with much muttering and open resentment. Their kin in neighboring towns took them in. This high-handed eviction left Coronado and his crew snug winter accommodations as well as storerooms bulging with native foodstuffs. But it also alienated the Tiwas and pointed them on the road that eventually led to armed struggle.

As gales howled among bare limbs of the cottonwoods and the surface of the river gradually froze to a brittle hardness, unrest in Tiguex grew. The sons of Spain had large appetites and soon they were making levies on other pueblos for additional supplies. Some trifled with Indian women, and all caused general offense by their arrogant swagger and boorish manner.

The Tiwas struck back. A war party attacked the Spaniards' horse herd, wounded a guard, and made away with a number of animals. A pursuit squad under one of Coronado's junior officers trailed the stolen stock downriver to the pueblo of Alameda, located on the northern outskirts of modern Albuquerque. The village was deserted, but several dead horses bristling with arrows were found. Riding back to report to their commander, the men passed another pueblo called Arenal. Inside the walls they could hear a great commotion where more of the stolen horses were being slaughtered.

The report delivered to Coronado was grim: the people of Tiguex were in open rebellion. At a council of war attended by the officers and chaplains of the expedition an agreement was reached to punish the Indians by force of arms.

Coronado ordered out his troops, and like avenging crusaders they marched to the conquest of Arenal. In a bloody and furious battle lasting many hours, they sacked and burned the pueblo. Some of the defenders were lanced to death or trampled under pounding hooves as they attempted to flee. Others taken captive were promptly tied to stakes and roasted alive. The few who escaped spread a message of terror across the land: the Spanish intruders were pitiless in battle, merciless in victory. That somber word was given further credence a short time later when Coronado's army laid siege to the pueblo of Moho, four leagues from Alcanfor, capturing it only after many of its inhabitants had perished from thirst.

As a result of these hostilities, the Province of Tiguex suffered almost total devastation. The remaining pueblos were abandoned as their people sought refuge in the mountains far from the bullets and blades of their enemies. It was a disaster from which the Indians of the Middle Rio Grande Valley would never fully recover, and one they would never entirely forget.

Spring came late in 1541. On April 23 of that year the Spanish army walked its horses across the still solid ice covering the Rio Grande and headed east to continue the quest for the Golden Fleece. The residents of Tiguex were thereby granted an interval of peace in which they could begin putting their shattered pueblos back together. The respite proved all too brief.

A little over a month after taking up the trail anew, Coronado reached the center of the awesome Staked Plains in the Texas Panhandle. There, concluding that prospects for some major discovery looked dim, he sent the main expedition under Captain Alvarado back to New Mexico. With thirty select stalwarts to serve him as an escort, he pressed ahead. His reconnaissance eventually led to Quivira, the home of the Wichita Indians in central Kansas. But to the eyes of the treasure-hungry Spaniards, it had even less to offer than the lands already visited. The poverty of Quivira dashed their last hopes for glory and wealth.

Meanwhile, retracing his steps to the Rio Grande, Alvarado found that the Tiwas, hearing of his approach, had taken to the hills again, leaving their province deserted. Without opposition, he reoccupied the pueblo of Alcanfor. But unlike the previous winter, the storerooms were now empty. If starvation were not to overtake the expedition during the hard months ahead, new supplies would have to be found. To this end, Captain Alvarado began ranging up and down the Rio Grande demanding contributions of food in other Pueblo districts. The Spaniards' reputation for harshness had preceded them, so the provisions sought were furnished quickly, though grudgingly. Therefore, when Coronado, finishing his bootless errand to Quivira, arrived back at Alcanfor in September, he found enough supplies on hand to see them through until spring.

After weathering another frigid and uncomfortable winter, the disillusioned Coronado ordered the trumpets sounded and pointed his face toward home. So it was farewell to New Mexico for the Spaniards, at least for the time being, and it was good-bye to uninvited and thoroughly quarrelsome guests for the embittered natives of Tiguex. The entire enterprise, costing so much money, lost lives, and human suffering, served no other purpose than to acquaint European mapmakers, who studied the expedition's chronicles, with the geography of interior North America. It also had the effect, unrecognized at the time, of indelibly engraving Coronado's name upon the pages of southwestern history. It is one of the small ironies of that history that the man who led this fiasco and whose expensive expedition returned not one centavo of profit should have his name, four centuries later, attached to New Mexico's largest shopping mall. Albuquerque's multimillion-dollar Coronado Center commemorates the region's first entrepreneur, a man who went broke.

Over the next forty years, the Pueblos of the Middle Rio Grande Valley slipped back into that unhurried, familiar rhythm of life they had known before the fire-eating Spaniards turned their small world upside-down. They remained free from outside meddling during that time largely because no one in the Viceroyalty of New Spain felt any inclination to retrace Coronado's trail. More than a generation would pass, dimming the unpleasant memories of his expedition, before Europeans again looked to New Mexico as a Promised Land.

Beginning in 1581, a series of new ventures launched from the south opened the next chapter in the history of the Tiwa Pueblos and the Albuquerque area. First, a small party of three priests escorted by nine soldiers, under the leadership of Fray Agustín Rodríguez, marched up the Rio Grande to examine the possibilities of initiating missionary work among the Indians. One of the fathers was killed by the Pueblos when he improvidently set out alone to carry reports back to Mexico. The remaining two, Fray Agustín and his companion Fray Francisco López, elected to stay in New Mexico at the conclusion of the tour, seeing, through rose-colored glasses, a horde of waiting converts. Either because of ignorance or carelessness, they picked the unlikeliest Pueblo group upon which to bestow their attentions, the Tiwas. Settling in at the village of Puaray, a short distance southeast of Alcanfor, Rodríguez and López met death very soon after the departure of their soldier guards. In the shedding of the friars' blood, the Indians exacted a small measure of retribution for the monumental miseries heaped upon them four decades before by Coronado.

The following year, 1582, another body of Spaniards, this one led by an adventurer, Antonio de Espejo, journeyed to New Mexico, ostensibly to learn the fate of the pair of missionaries left in Tiguex. Upon finding that the padres had perished, Espejo showed his true motive in coming. Prospecting was his game and for several months he scoured the sunbleached hills and mesas for sign of gold or silver.

In his official report of the expedition, Antonio de Espejo tells us that Tiguex contained sixteen pueblos and that its people, through sign language, gave him a vivid account of their earlier troubles with Coronado. Many of the Indians, relates Espejo, thought that he had come to punish them for killing the friars, and in panic they skipped to the Sandias to hide. "We tried by all means possible," his report continues, "to persuade them to come back peacefully, but they refused. . . . We were unable to find out how many inhabitants there were, because they had fled."

In 1591, still a third expedition entered New Mexico. The commander was Gaspar Castaño de Sosa. With him came families and wagons of supplies, for it was his intention to found a settlement among the Pueblos. The Tiwas, living in the shadow of the Sandias, he observed, were skittish as deer and fled at his approach. All their past experience seemed to confirm that the presence of the Spaniards spelled nothing but trouble.

Castaño de Sosa's plan of establishing a foothold on the Rio Grande came to nothing. He had embarked on the undertaking without the necessary government authorization, and soon after his arrival in New Mexico, a military force dispatched by the viceroy suddenly appeared with an order for his arrest. He and his would-be settlers were escorted home. The Pueblos breathed a fresh sigh of relief.

The brief visits of Rodríguez, Espejo, and Castaño de Sosa had little impact on the Middle Rio Grande Valley. From them, the Indians might have divined that Spanish penetration into their homeland was destined to grow. But the ephemeral nature of these early contacts scarcely prepared the native people for the cultural shock and psychological stresses they would experience when European colonization and evangelization got under way.

Don Juan de Oñate, governor and captain-general of the newly proclaimed Kingdom of New Mexico, was the individual who fastened Spain's hold on the land of the Pueblos. Journeying northward from his native Zacatecas at the head of a slow-moving caravan of colonists and missionaries, he entered the Province of Tiguex in late June of 1598, as the first ears of Indian corn were beginning to form on the stalk. Hard rains greeted his arrival and at one point he and his people got mired in the mud as they were crossing one of the many grain fields that lined both banks of the river. Oñate paused briefly at Puaray Pueblo, noting solemnly in his journal that there the venerable Fathers Rodríguez and López had given up their lives.

The governor was searching for a suitable site upon

which his subjects could create a town and he could establish his military headquarters and political capital. At first glance, the valley containing the Tiwa pueblos appeared ideal. The country was open and gave easy access to the trail south. And the wide bottomlands abutting the river were obviously fertile and simple to irrigate.

But other, negative considerations outweighed those positive points. For one, the Indian farms flanking the dozen or more pueblos already had most of the available ground under cultivation, and, as Oñate well knew, Spanish law carried strict provisions for protection of native lands. In any case, it was apparent that the Tiwas would have made churlish neighbors. Their previous meetings with Spaniards had left them distrustful and fearful, and certainly in no mood to welcome a community of these outlanders in their midst.

Juan de Oñate was in fact aware of the Tiwas' deep-seated hostility and he also knew, from reading the reports of earlier expeditions, that the Indians farther north, who had had less contact with Spaniards, possessed a friendlier disposition. Moreover, the same reports spoke of good mining prospects in the northern mountains, and the governor thought it best to have his new town close by any gold or silver mines that might be discovered. For these compelling reasons, he did not stop and settle in the Middle Valley of the Rio Grande. Instead, from Puaray, he continued upriver to the Española Valley, and there raised his capital of San Gabriel not far from the Tewa pueblo of San Juan.

During New Mexico's infant years as a new realm of the Spanish Empire, no settlers took up residence on or near the future site of Albuquerque. But there was much coming and going of travelers and supply caravans, since the Middle Valley lay athwart the main north-south road, or Camino Real, as it came to be called. Actually, the first people to show an authentic interest in the area were missionaries, not colonists.

Soon after setting up housekeeping in the Española Valley, Oñate divided up the band of Franciscan friars, which had accompanied him, assigning individuals to minister to the various groups of pueblos. Father Juan Carlos drew the southern Tiwas. He moved into one of the larger villages, probably Puaray, and began trying to win the Indians to Christianity. As far as the records show, he built no mission and, in fact, within a few years gave up his efforts.

Don Pedro de Peralta, Oñate's successor as governor, arrived in New Mexico in 1609. Almost at once, he abandoned San Gabriel and commenced laying the foundations for a new capital at Santa Fe, whose location, near the foot of the Sangre de Cristo Mountains, was deemed better suited to the needs of the growing colony. At the same time, the Spanish Crown began showing a more active interest in promoting the missionary program as a means to "civilize" and assimilate the Pueblo Indians. With considerable financial support from the government, the Church launched a massive drive to convert the native people and to erect more than a score of majestic missions throughout the region.

Two of the new churches were placed among the Tiwa, one at Sandia Pueblo and another at Isleta. Both had extensive auxiliary buildings, which included priests' quarters, workshops, and classrooms. Of the two missions, Father Alonso de Benavides wrote in 1630: "There are schools of reading and writing, singing, and playing all instruments. The pupils are well taught in Church doctrine and ways of civilized living. These two monasteries and churches are very costly and beautiful." From other documents, we learn that each place had its own organ, the melodious strains of which must have sounded strange indeed to the Indians, whose only instruments were drums, rattles, and flutes.

A pair of lesser missions, referred to as *visitas*, were constructed at the pueblos of Puaray and Alameda. Initially, at least, they had no resident missionary of their own, but were served periodically by the padres stationed at Sandia. Alameda, in the 1660s, got its own minister, but continued to remain a mission of secondary importance.

Statistical information for the seventeenth century is extremely sketchy and unreliable, but from the data available, it would appear that the Tiwa populations steadily declined. The same phenomenon was noticeable everywhere among the Pueblos of New Mexico and can be linked to the introduction of measles, smallpox, and other Old World diseases by the Europeans. Lacking any natural immunity to such maladies, the Indians succumbed in droves with each recurring epidemic. As their numbers dwindled in the many small and scattered pueblos, the survivors tended to congregate in fewer, but larger, communities. By the second half of the seventeenth century, the southern Tiwas had deserted practically all their outlying villages and joined their kinsmen clustered in the four pueblos of Sandia, Isleta, Alameda, and Puaray.

As this decline and concentration of the native population occurred, vacant Indian farmlands throughout the Middle Valley became available to Hispanic settlers. After the early

1650s, increasing numbers of colonists from the upper portion of the province, as well as new immigrants, obtained rural properties, or estancias, in this area. By the mid-1660s, such estancias seem to have numbered several dozen. Their residents attended church at the nearest Indian mission and journeyed to Santa Fe on periodic business trips or for social occasions. The capital, in fact, remained the realm's only formally organized municipality in the years before the Pueblo Revolt of 1680.

Although no real community existed in the Middle Valley, the region had its own *alcalde mayor*, or district magistrate, who handled minor judicial cases and measured the boundaries of land grants assigned by the governor. The office was customarily filled by one of the local *estancieros*. About 1660 it became the practice to divide New Mexico into two major subdivisions or administrative units—the Rio Arriba and the Rio Abajo, that is, the upper and lower portions of the Rio Grande Valley, together with neighboring districts. The dividing line between the two was the high east-west escarpment known as La Bajada, situated about twenty miles below Santa Fe. The lieutenant governor of New Mexico was given direct command of the Rio Abajo, mainly to handle a growing problem there with hostile Apaches. The governor focused his attention on affairs in the northern district.

In those early years, most of the Spanish estancias of the Rio Abajo were concentrated in two principal areas. The first was located toward the head of the valley, near The Narrows of the Rio Grande, and on the border between the Tiwa and Keres pueblos, which was between the mouth of the Jemez River and San Felipe. The Spanish folk spoke of this locality as La Angostura de Bernalillo, meaning The Narrows of Little Bernal. The Bernal family lived thereabouts, and doubtless the diminutive, Bernalillo, derived from their name.

Somewhere in this quarter, the governor of New Mexico in 1643 established a temporary military post, the presidio of San Antonio, to guard a ford on the Rio Grande frequented by Apache raiders. The garrison consisted of one captain and fifteen soldiers. This defensive experiment must have been short-lived, for the San Antonio fort received only a single passing mention in documents of the period.

Among those who carved out estates around The Narrows of Bernalillo were, in addition to the Bernals, such prominent families as the Bacas, Carvajals, Cuéllars, Sáenzes, Pereas, and Anayas. The mere listing of names tells us nothing about the people themselves, their tight-knit society, or the kind of life they led on their largely self-sufficient estancias. Information of this kind, which might have been recorded on paper, was almost entirely lost when the Pueblo Indians unleashed their holy war against New Mexico in 1680.

About one of the Bernalillo settlers, however, some fragmentary details have survived, mainly because his haughty and unconventional ways led to his trial and imprisonment by the Inquisition in Mexico City. His name was Cristóbal de Anaya, and he was born in New Mexico in the late 1620s. Descended from grandparents who were natives of the Spanish city of Salamanca, Cristóbal had no claim to nobility, but that did not prevent him from building a career and putting on airs that were typical of many blue bloods of the day. At the tender age of eleven, so the records inform us, he took up soldiering, a fact less astounding when we recall that frontier youth matured early, and often assumed the responsibilities of manhood before the onset of adolescence.

By his mid-thirties, fiery Cristóbal de Anaya was embroiled in the intense factional squabbles that characterized colonial New Mexican politics. Evidently, he took the side of civil officials who attempted to curb the immense power of the missionary fathers, and this partisanship may well have contributed to his ensuing troubles with the Church. In 1661, he was arrested by agents of the Inquisition, for supposedly heretical remarks, and sent to Mexico City, in chains, we assume, since that was the practice then.

For four miserable years, Cristóbal remained confined in the Inquisition's dungeons, undergoing a series of trials. At last he was forced to march in a procession of penitents through the streets of the viceregal capital, as a token of his humiliation. Subsequently he was released. All things considered, he got off gently.

Back in New Mexico, among wife and children on his estancia at Angostura, Cristóbal de Anaya made light of the hardships suffered at the hands of the Inquisition. The experience seems to have taught him little, for shortly he resumed his old habit of speaking disrespectfully of the Church. One priest even brought charges against him, but this time the matter was not followed up. Before many more years passed, he and his family were to fall victim to the rage of the Pueblos, as our narrative will soon show.

The other focal point of Spanish activity in the Middle Valley lay south of Sandia and Alameda pueblos, extending downriver past the future site of Albuquerque to the boundary marking the lands of the Isleta Indians. By the middle

1660s, twenty or more estancias existed in this area, which together with those to the north made a total of about forty-five estates for the entire valley. The main houses on many of these properties were referred to as haciendas, suggesting a rather spacious and commodious dwelling. But in truth, we know from archaeological and documentary evidence that most of the residences were of fairly modest size, and we can guess that comforts and anything approaching luxurious furnishing must have been few.

Names of the owners of several of these haciendas, within or close by modern Albuquerque, are of considerable importance to the early history of the district. One was Alonso García de Noriega who in his early twenties had come to New Mexico from Zacatecas and begun developing lands, called the Estancia de San Antonio, on the west bank of the Rio Grande. He is mentioned in 1670 as being the local alcalde mayor, and ten years later he had become lieutenant-governor, ruling over the entire Rio Abajo and holding the military rank of *maese de campo* (equivalent to lieutenant-general). His hacienda, no doubt among the foremost of such establishments, sheltered a wife and numerous children.

Approximately opposite Alonso García's property was the house of Francisco de Trujillo, on the east side of the river. Unlike his prosperous neighbor, the lieutenant governor, Señor Trujillo, so far as is known, had no titles and little wealth. Evidently he died sometime in the 1670s, leaving the home to his wife. Thereafter, the place was known as the Hacienda de Doña Luisa de Trujillo, and formed the site upon which Albuquerque would be founded in 1706.

Doña Luisa's name was attached not only to her hacienda

but also to the great stand of cottonwoods that thrived in the surrounding lowlands. Far into the following century, long after the woman herself had been forgotten and the hacienda had crumbled to dust, the trees continued to be known as the Bosque Grande de Doña Luisa. An alternate name for the grove, at least in the beginning, seems to have been the Bosque Grande de San Francisco Xavier, in honor of the patron saint of the locality.

The house of Francisco de Trujillo and Doña Luisa lay near the southern end of the cottonwood forest, for the next place below, the Hacienda de Mejía, was said in 1692 to be situated in open pastureland without trees. Much of this area, now within south Albuquerque, comprised swamps and shallow pools and was known as the Esteros de Mejía. The founder and developer of the hacienda was presumably named Mejía, but since no such family appears in the records of the day, it is possible that the owner, whoever he may have been, borrowed the name of the nearby swamp for his house. In any case, the Hacienda de Mejía was located square beside the Camino Real and was a designated *paraje,* which meant that it was a spot where travelers customarily stopped for the night. That fact alone lent it added significance.

The Spanish colonists, dispersed on their estancias throughout the valley, must have felt keenly the lack of churches and communities of their own. The padres at the neighboring Indian missions could provide them the sacraments, but their interests and energies were directed mainly toward the Pueblos, not the settlers. Spaniards have an almost hereditary affinity for town life, with its round of religious observances, public markets, and social activity centered upon a plaza, all supported by a municipal political structure based on accumulated tradition. Formal creation of new communities was one of the first steps taken by the sixteenth-century conquistadores as they expanded the limits of New Spain.

Just why the Spaniards failed to establish a legal settlement in the Middle Valley prior to 1680 cannot be satisfactorily explained. The interest was there and one or more feeble attempts were made to do so, but they came to nothing. For example, in 1662, Governor Diego de Peñalosa traveled down from Santa Fe and at a meeting held on the estancia of Pedro Varela (or Barela) de Losada he drew up an order calling for the creation of a formal town, or *villa*. Twelve to fifteen persons, who agreed to participate in the venture, affixed their names to the document along with the governor. The Varela estate is believed to have been somewhere inside present-day Albuquerque, perhaps within the area of the south valley now known as Las Barelas.

It is apparent that Governor Peñalosa as well as other prominent men of the day regarded the country along the Rio Grande between Sandia and Isleta as the best possible site in all New Mexico for establishment of a new town. But neither he nor his immediate successors in the governorship were able to bring about such a project. We can only suppose that their attention was diverted by the multitude of problems that plagued the province during the third quarter of the seventeenth century.

The most serious of these was the growing discontent and belligerence of the Pueblo Indians. In 1650, several villages formed a league with the Apaches for the purpose of rebellion. They planned to attack on the night of Holy Thursday when the Spaniards were assembled in the churches and would be defenseless. The plot, however, was discovered and nine ringleaders were hanged, including several Tiwas from the pueblos of Alameda and Sandia. Although this first attempt at a general uprising fizzled, the seeds of resistance had been sown. Over the next three decades, hostile incidents multiplied at an alarming rate and should have sounded a clear and frightening warning to the colonists that they were in for rough sledding. But like most people, they preferred to live with their comfortable illusions rather than face facts, and so the signs of coming disaster went largely ignored.

The great Pueblo Revolt, when it broke forth with noise and fury in the summer of 1680, was sparked by multiple causes that had flowed together over the years to form a single well of bitterness among the Indians. Their largest complaint against the rulers of the land was directed at the padres, who, since the arrival of Oñate, had worked with fierce dedication to stamp out native religion. That religion, supported by an elaborate ceremonialism, permeated every aspect of the Indians' daily life, and to give it up, as the missionaries demanded, threatened to destroy not only the social and political structure of each village, but also the sense of world order and personal identity of the individual.

The Spanish fathers, operating within the framework of medieval Christianity, were inflexible and obdurate. The old pagan religion, a product of the Devil, they believed, had to go—in its entirety. No room existed for compromise. With Spanish soldiers backing them, they raided Indian kivas, burned the sacred masks and fetishes, and relentlessly persecuted the caciques, or native priests, whom they stigmatized as sorcerers.

Predictably, such heavy-handed abuse did not achieve the goal intended. The ancient rites went undercover, the new religion of the friars was discredited, and wrathful indignation was kindled in the breast of the oppressed Pueblos.

From about 1660 onward, drought followed by famine added to the Indians' woes. In this calamity, they saw a direct connection with the work of the meddling padres: the traditional ceremonies, many of them devoted to rainmaking, were increasingly disrupted by outside interference, and the visible result was a withering away of summer showers and winter snows. The Pueblos concluded that if the missionary program continued unchecked, they would eventually perish.

But the Indians' displeasure was not directed solely at the friars. They had a strong case, too, against Spanish settlers and officials who, in violation of royal laws, habitually exploited the native people. Several Pueblo witnesses gave testimony, after the Revolt, as to their motives and the nature of their grievances. They spoke of beatings, theft of property, violation of their women. At those seasons of the year when they were most needed in their own fields, Spanish landowners had forced them to work on the estancias. Often they had not even been paid for this labor, as the law required. Among those accused of gross misconduct was the lieutenant governor himself, Alonso García.

Given the gravity of the complaints, it is hardly surprising that New Mexico's Pueblo Indians were driven to desperate measures. Under a shining bowl of blue sky, they raised the banner of rebellion throughout the land on August 10, 1680. Within a few days, most of the bloody work was done. Of the 32 missionaries in the province, 21 died. Among the colonists, 380 men, women, and children lost their lives, some in isolated estancias, others on the road where they were overtaken in flight. The retribution meted out was as merciless as it was widespread.

In the north, those settlers in the countryside who managed to escape hurried to Santa Fe, where the governor, Antonio de Otermín, rallied the survivors behind the fortified walls of his adobe palace. Besieged, the residents of the capital held out for ten days while Otermín tried in vain to get a messenger through to Lieutenant-governor García in the south, asking for aid. At last, when no help was forthcoming, the Spaniards gathered up what they could, abandoned their city, and fled down the course of the Rio Grande.

Reaching the head of the Middle Valley at La Angostura, the benumbed refugees were greeted by a picture of desolation and horror. Estancia after estancia lay sacked and destroyed, the gutted haciendas containing the mangled corpses of owners and workers. At the once proud house of Captain Cristóbal de Anaya, he who had defied the Church and suffered a trial before the Inquisition, Governor Otermín paused long enough to record in his journal the grim findings: buildings looted, all the livestock run off, and the naked bodies of the Captain, his wife, six children, and servants scattered before the main door.

Continuing downriver, the Spaniards reached Sandia Pueblo. They found it empty, its people gone. The church and cells of the friars had been ransacked. The retreating Indians left a carved full-length figure of Saint Francis on the altar, its arm hacked off by an ax. Vestments and sacred vessels had been profaned with human excrement. And wheat straw was piled on the floor of the church and in the choir loft where it had been left ablaze. Otermín seemingly made no attempt to extinguish the fire, preferring to renew his march at once.

A short distance below the pueblo, a body of armed Tiwas appeared in the foothills skirting the road and commenced firing at the forlorn cavalcade. The governor brought his people to a halt and ordered fifty men out to engage the enemy. The Indians quickly faded into the furrowed slopes of the Sandia Mountains, driving with them a great herd of cattle and horses plundered from the mission and estancias. Otermín, casting a glance over his shoulder, observed a huge column of smoke issuing from the Sandia church. That sight, as much as the Tiwa attack, prompted him to send a party back with instructions to fire the entire pueblo. Given the magnitude of the disaster that had already befallen him, it was a comparatively small retaliatory gesture. But it carried a sting nevertheless, especially for the population of Sandia, which was left homeless.

At the next pueblo, Alameda, the Spaniards obtained a bit of welcome news. From an old Indian found hiding in a cornfield, it was learned that Lieutenant-governor García and other colonists had survived, and believing everyone at Santa Fe to have perished, they were then on the road below Socorro, headed out of New Mexico. Otermín at once dispatched a squad of four men to overtake García with orders for him to stop until the governor's convoy could catch up.

Leaving Alameda, Otermín marched to the estancia of Doña Luisa de Trujillo, three leagues away. En route his army passed in sight of the ruined hacienda of Alonso García on the west bank of the Rio Grande. Four leagues below Doña Luisa's house, they came to the shell of the Gómez hacienda. There the governor entered a brief note in his journal: "All along this road from the pueblo of Sandia to this estancia everything was found deserted and pillaged, alike of cattle and of household possessions, there being many haciendas on both sides of the river, all of which were sacked and destroyed by the enemy." Much of the country of which he was speaking is now encompassed within the sprawling boundaries of Albuquerque.

Farther south, Otermín was at last able to unite his force with that of García and together they proceeded to El Paso. There a government in exile was established to await the time when upper New Mexico could be reconquered. The governor attempted that very thing himself late the following year, 1681.

Raising a small army, he set out with a blare of trumpets and rode north to Isleta, the first pueblo he found inhabited. Governor Otermín had expected to see the Indians remorseful and if not eager, at least willing, to be received back into the fold of Spanish Church and state. The bellicose and unrepentant attitude of the Isletas, however, swiftly dispelled that unrealistic hope. As Father Francisco de Ayeta, who accompanied the expedition, wrote, "They have been found to be so pleased with liberty of conscience and so attached to the belief in the worship of Satan that up to the present not a sign has been visible of their ever having been Christians."

Venturing on, the Spaniards visited the Tiwa villages of Alameda, Puaray, and Sandia, the last having been rebuilt since its burning the previous year. Because the residents of all three had fled at his approach, Otermín took it upon himself to fire the villages, the only act of punishment of which he was capable. But with that deed, really a symbol of the governor's frustration, it was apparent that New Mexico was not to be reconquered, at least for the present. On giving up the project and withdrawing to El Paso, he paused at Isleta long enough to put the pueblo to the torch and carry away 385 of its inhabitants as prisoners.

For the next decade, the Pueblo Indians held on to their independence, enjoying that liberty of conscience that Father Ayeta had found so repugnant. But all the while, the Spaniards at El Paso were assembling men and supplies against the day when they could return and reclaim New Mexico. To carry out that much-desired mission, the Spanish Crown appointed a new governor in 1691, Don Diego de Vargas Zapata y Luján. In August of the following year, he embarked for Santa Fe with a strong force at his back, intending to make a thorough reconnaissance of the land and, if possible, to win back the Pueblos through peaceful persuasion.

Traveling with an escort in advance of his main army, Vargas passed the bleak and burned-out walls of Isleta and arrived at the ruined hacienda of Mejía. A brief survey showed the site to be plentifully furnished with water and good pasture, so he decided, as soon as his wagons arrived, to create a supply base there. In writing of this decision, he declared, "I leave at this place and hacienda called Mejía, Rafael Téllez Jirón, whom I appoint as campaign captain and leader of the camp. He is to be in charge of guarding and defending the stores which I leave in reserve at this hacienda, and also the cattle, oxen, and horses." In thus ridding himself of excess baggage, Vargas gained greater mobility for his troops, an important advantage should he be obliged to fight at the portals of Santa Fe.

Happily for the Spaniards, that prospect was avoided. At

the capital they discovered a large population of Pueblos occupying Otermín's old palace and neighboring buildings in the center of town. After lengthy discussions, a truce was arranged allowing Vargas and his soldiers to enter the courtyard of the palace. There the governor raised the royal banner, shouted "Long live our king, Carlos the Second!" and proclaimed New Mexico once again under the rule of Spain. His men joyfully tossed their hats in the air and the chaplains fell on their knees to give thanks for their good fortune.

A significant first step had been taken, but much remained to be done. The far reaches of Puebloland had to be pacified. To that end, Vargas led his troops from one side of New Mexico to the other, addressing each pueblo in turn, as well as stray bands of Navajos and Apaches met on the road, urging submission. Responses varied from polite compliance to sullen silence. But the governor felt that in the main his errand was a huge success. With that, he guided his army back to El Paso.

Once there, Vargas began preparations to return upriver with a full contingent of settlers and missionaries, so that the province might be effectively repopulated. Some of the people who had survived the 1680 disaster were still in El Paso, ready to go and rebuild their homes. Their number was insufficient, however, for the large work the governor had in mind, and hence he set off on a quick trip to his native city of Zacatecas in central Mexico to launch a recruiting program.

By the fall of 1693, when Vargas departed El Paso for Santa Fe, his expedition boasted more than eight hundred persons, including seventeen missionaries. As the cavalcade passed through the Middle Valley, on its way northward, the governor gave some of the colonists permission to drop out in the vicinity of Alameda and Sandia and begin establishing homes. Presumably, most of these were old settlers who had lived there before the revolt.

At Santa Fe, the Spaniards got a rude shock. Many of the Indians who had submitted the year before, now repudiated their allegiance and showed they were prepared to open a new war. The Pueblos still holding the capital resisted Vargas's entry and had to be expelled in a wild and bloody battle. Then, over the succeeding months, rebellious Indians in outlying areas were brought to bay in a series of campaigns that sapped Vargas's physical strength as well as his material resources. That he prevailed in the end was owing principally to help obtained from certain pueblos that remained friendly and provided him with auxiliary warriors who marched and fought alongside his own troops.

By early 1695, the governor had matters well enough in hand that he could write the viceroy of New Spain and exclaim exuberantly, "With sails full we forge ahead." His confidence was buoyed by arrival of his second-in-command, Lieutenant-governor Juan Páez Hurtado, with more settlers, soldiers, and supplies from the south. Now he had the wherewithal to begin founding new towns. That was an aim uppermost in his mind, because Vargas knew that until New Mexico possessed more municipalities to serve as strongholds and symbols of Spanish power, it would remain vulnerable to the kind of rebellion that had swept over the province in 1680.

The first town he formed was the villa of Santa Cruz de la Cañada, just east of modern Española. Taking sixty-six of the recently arrived families, he rode north from Santa Fe on

April 21, 1695, and placed them in possession of the new site. Since this was a frontier town, it was provided with a military government composed of an alcalde mayor, a captain of militia, and assorted junior officers. Settlers were given seeds, farm implements, and firearms. With this kind of support, Governor Vargas hoped that Santa Cruz would become the main bastion of Spanish defense north of Santa Fe.

Later the same year, he moved to create a similar protective bulwark in the south with the founding of Bernalillo. Details surrounding the town's birth are murky, but this much can be said: a group of colonists laid out a plaza and built a church and friary dedicated to San Francisco, at a site several miles north of present-day Bernalillo, and probably on the west side of the Rio Grande. The place became the residence of an alcalde mayor (the first being Fernando Durán y Chávez) who, initially at least, had jurisdiction over the entire Middle Valley. Roundabout, land grants were made to individuals who carved out ranchos, or small farmsteads. These took the place of the grand estancias that had characterized rural life in the valley before the revolt. The shift to landholdings of more modest size was due in part to the fact that lands were now to be cultivated primarily by farmers and their families, rather than by enforced Pueblo labor, as had been the practice before 1680. The government believed that the old system, with its assorted abuses, had helped stir up rebellion among the Indians.

While Bernalillo was the first regular community developed in the Middle Valley, and the focal point of Spanish activity there during the final five years of the seventeenth century, settlers lost no time in applying for land grants and filling in the country south as far as the swamps of Mejía. One of their number was a man named Pedro López, who received a grant from the hand of Governor Vargas, dated March 4, 1695. The location of this farm, which López called San Nicolás, was described as being "opposite the agricultural lands of Atrisco and on the edge of the Esteros de Mejía." Thus, the property was very close to the lands upon which Albuquerque would be founded eleven years later.

Some confusion exists about the municipal status of Bernalillo during its first years. It is mentioned briefly in 1696 as the Real de Bernalillo, the term *real* being the legal title for a mining town. Several small mines were operated fitfully in colonial times at the north end of the Sandia Mountains, and perhaps it was in anticipation that that area would become a major mineral producer that led to Bernalillo's original designation as a real. Be that as it may, the title quickly fell by the wayside and was heard of no more. Father Juan Alvarez, in preparing a summary report of New Mexico communities and missions in 1706, referred to the town as the Villa de Bernalillo. Now, a villa, under Spanish law, was a fully chartered town with specific rights and privileges extended to it by the crown. Santa Fe was a villa, as was Santa Cruz de la Cañada founded by Vargas in 1695. But in no other document known can we find confirmation of Alvarez's statement that such a rank was bestowed upon Bernalillo. One can only conclude that the good friar made a slip of the pen while preparing his report. In documents of the early eighteenth century, Bernalillo is most often cited as a *puesto*—in Spanish, literally, a "place," but in New Mexico it had the special meaning of a "small town."

If Bernalillo owned any signal claim to fame during its first decade of life, it came from a melancholy event that transpired there on April 8, 1704. The previous month Governor Vargas, then sixty years of age and worn thin by hard service, had set out with fifty Spanish soldiers and a contingent of Pueblo warriors to pursue hostile Apaches who had been raiding in the Middle Rio Grande Valley. Riding out from Santa Fe, he had chosen Bernalillo as his military headquarters and base of operations for the campaign.

From there he headed the main force downriver while his scouts ranged through the heights of the Sandias and Manzanos looking for signs of the enemy. Suddenly, some miles south of the site of Albuquerque, the governor fell deathly ill. Alarmed, his officers called a halt to the expedition and retreated hastily to Bernalillo with their ailing commander. The alcalde mayor, Don Fernando Durán y Chávez, took Vargas into his home. Realizing that death was at hand, the governor called for a quill and paper and beginning with the words, "In the name of God Almighty," wrote his last will and testament. Therein, he ordered that a mass be said for his soul in the Bernalillo church, with the body present, and that afterward the corpse be conveyed to Santa Fe for burial. Don Fernando and his eldest son, Bernardo, were among those who signed the will as witnesses. Scarcely had the document been composed when Don Diego de Vargas died. The passing of New Mexico's reconqueror marked the end of an era.

FIG. I.

Looking toward the Rio Grande
Valley and Sandia Mountains, 1941,
before Albuquerque suburbs had
spread over the East and West
Mesas. Old U.S. Highway 66 in the
center. (State Records Center and
Archives, Santa Fe, DOD Collection)

**Fig. 2.**

Geography of the
Albuquerque Area

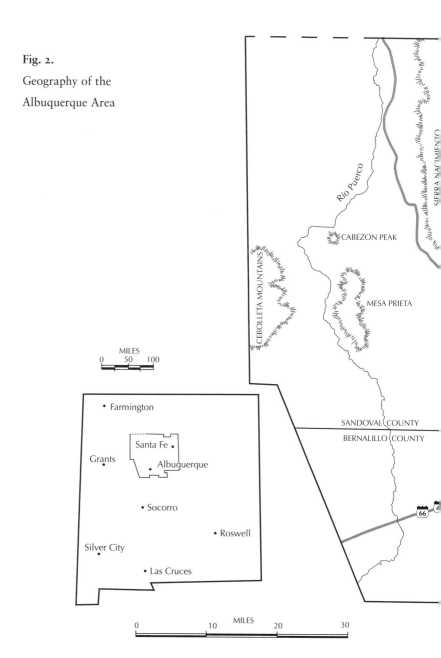

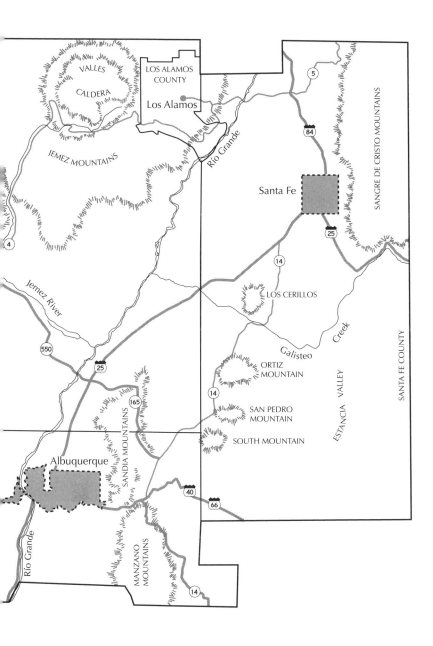

VALLES

CALDERA

LOS ALAMOS
COUNTY

Los Alamos

JEMEZ MOUNTAINS

Río Grande

SANGRE DE CRISTO MOUNTAINS

5

84

Santa Fe

25

14

Jemez River

LOS CERILLOS

Galisteo

Creek

550

ORTIZ
MOUNTAIN

25

SANTA FE COUNTY

165

14

SAN PEDRO
MOUNTAIN

ESTANCIA VALLEY

Albuquerque

SANDIA MOUNTAINS

SOUTH MOUNTAIN

40

66

Río Grande

MANZANO
MOUNTAINS

14

4

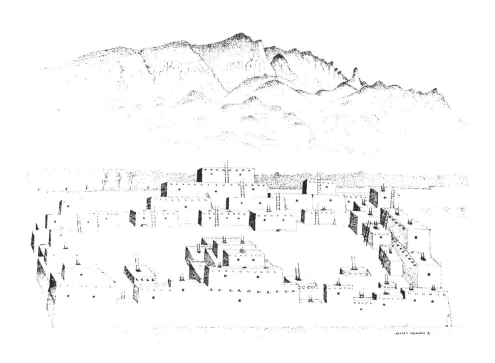

**Fig. 3.**
Artist's conception of Kuaua in
1540. (Courtesy of El Palacio)

**Fig. 4.**

Zia Pueblo Mission, typical
of the churches built near
Albuquerque in the colonial period.
(From a painting by Carlos Vierra)

Fig. 5.

Pueblo Indian Dancers, from Report
on Indians Taxed: Eleventh U.S.
Census, 1890. (Photograph
courtesy of Marc Simmons)

**Fig. 6.**

Modern reenactors in the costumes of Coronado's soldiers.

(Photograph courtesy of Marc Simmons)

**Fig. 7.**
Don Francisco
Fernández de la Cueva
Enríquez, Duke of
Alburquerque, Viceroy
of New Spain,
1702–1711. (Courtesy
of El Palacio)

**Fig. 8.**
Signatures of
the Duke of
Alburquerque
and Francisco
Cuervo y Valdés.

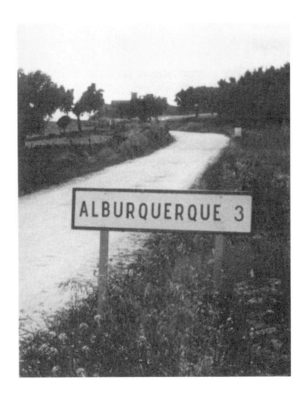

**Fig. 9.**

Road sign to Alburquerque, Spain.

(Photograph courtesy of John L. Kessell)

Fig. 10.

Spanish settlements in the Middle Rio Grande Valley, 1779.

(From a map by Bernardo de Miera y Pacheco)

**Fig. 11.**
Artist José Cisneros's conception of a
Spanish caravan on the Camino Real
between Albuquerque and El Paso.
(Original art owned by the
Museum of New Mexico)

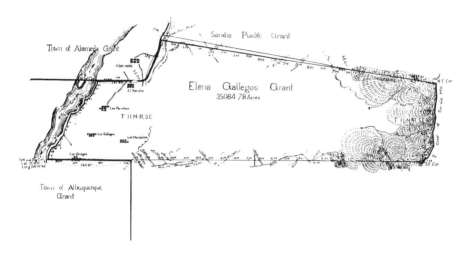

Fig. 12.

The Elena Gallegos Land Grant, 1897. Drawn by George
H. Pradl. (Courtesy of Special Collections, University of
New Mexico General Library, Catron Papers)

**Fig. 13.**

A period portrait of Governor Manuel Armijo, now owned by the
Albuquerque Museum. (Photograph courtesy of Marc Simmons)

Fig. 14.

Mexican period soldiers, reenactors in costume.

(Photograph courtesy of Marc Simmons)

# 2

# The Bosque Becomes a Villa

ON APRIL 23, 1706, seventy years before the American Revolution, Governor Francisco Cuervo y Valdés of New Mexico sat at a writing table in the dimly lit halls of his mud palace on the Santa Fe plaza. He was composing a formal document to his sovereign in Spain and to the viceroy in Mexico City, attesting to the creation of a new town. Deftly he wrote, "I certify to the king, our lord, and to the most excellent señor viceroy: That I founded a villa on the banks and in the valley of the Rio del Norte in a good place as regards land, water, pasture, and firewood. I gave it as patron saint the glorious apostle of the Indies, San Francisco Xavier, and called and named it the villa of Alburquerque."

With a hint of pride in his words, Governor Cuervo went on to relate the progress that had been made to date. Thirty-five families, he asserted, had already taken up residence in the town, comprising 252 adults and children. A spacious church had been completed and a house for the priest was well under way. A start had been made on the *casas reales*, that is, the government buildings for local officials. The settlers had finished their houses, which were provided with corrals for livestock. Irrigation ditches were open and running. Crops were sown. The town was in good order, well arranged, and all had been achieved without any expense to the Royal Treasury. This last implied that the people themselves had borne the entire costs for the town's founding.

The governor wished to emphasize the legality of his actions. Therefore, he declared that he had followed the procedures prescribed for the establishment of new municipalities as set forth in the royal laws contained in the *Recopilación*, the book of statutes that governed the conduct of colonial officials. Having said that, and having added a note attesting to the refounding of the Pueblo of Galisteo, which had been abandoned during the turbulence of the revolt and reconquest, Francisco Cuervo y Valdés affixed his signature to the paper, had it witnessed by his secretary, and sealed it with an impression of his coat of arms.

The governor's words contained in this formal document of certification seem straightforward and clear: he founded the villa of Albuquerque in 1706, he provided his superiors certain details about the number of settlers and the buildings then under construction or already completed, and he stated that the project had been carried out in strict conformity with the law. The legal code, which he referred to as the *Recopilación*, was the celebrated *Recopilación de Leyes de los Reynos de las Indias,* Spain's monumental compilation of laws covering practically all aspects of colonial government and public life. One section dealt specifically with the procedures and requirements for creation of new towns.

According to that code, a minimum of thirty family heads was necessary to charter a villa. The site chosen should have good water, arable land, and some timber, if possible. The town received as much land as needed, measured with a cord. At its center, space was to be marked off for a plaza, a church, and government buildings. As soon as streets were laid out, each family should be given a lot for a house and assigned farm plots in severalty. After living upon the lots and improving the farmland for a specified number of years, residents obtained final title. Portions of the town grant, not distributed to citizens, were reserved as commons *(ejidos)* available to all for pasturing, wood gathering, or rock quarrying. Further, a villa was to have an elected council *(cabildo)* with jurisdiction over executive and judicial affairs of the municipality. These major provisions, and other minor ones, were all designed to provide Spanish colonial towns with an orderly form of government.

Three days after certifying to the founding of Albuquerque, Governor Cuervo wrote a letter to Viceroy Francisco Fernández de la Cueva, Duke of Alburquerque. In it he provided background information about the new villa that had not been included in the earlier notice of certification. Motivated by a desire to see New Mexico expand and prosper, Governor Cuervo said that he had issued orders for the placing of a villa on the river below Bernalillo and Alameda. In advance of actual settlement, he had sent one of his subordinates, General Juan de Ulibarrí, to scout the area and find a suitable site. The site Ulibarrí selected possessed the necessary tillable land, water, pasture, and firewood, as the law required. It had other natural advantages, too, which though left unmentioned by Cuervo in his letter to the viceroy, could scarcely have escaped notice. For one, the center of the proposed villa was situated on ground slightly elevated above the surrounding bottom lands, affording some protection from periodic flooding by the Rio Grande, or Rio del Norte, as the governor called it. For another, the geographical position of the town appeared ideal as far as the practical needs of the future settlers were concerned. It lay astride the Camino Real, a good ford on the river existed near to the west, and a dozen miles due eastward yawned the mouth of the Cañon de Carnué (Tijeras Canyon), a pass giving access to the plains beyond the Sandia Mountains.

Once the site had been chosen, Cuervo explained that he made a public announcement throughout the province inviting citizens to join in creating the new community. Many families responded, he told the viceroy, bringing with them herds of cattle and flocks of sheep. For security, he detached a squad of ten soldiers from the Santa Fe presidio and sent it to escort the settlers while on the road and then take up permanent guard duty at the villa. The troops, accompanied by their families, were led by Captain Martín Hurtado. Their presence played an important part in attracting participants to the endeavor, because as the governor himself noted gravely, the country south of Bernalillo was alive with hostile Apaches. Even as few as ten soldiers stationed in the villa could offer considerable comfort to the Spanish colonists.

Thus far Governor Cuervo had provided the viceroy with simple information, but now he could not resist the temptation to make an optimistic forecast about his municipal creation. "I do not doubt, very excellent lord, that in a short time this will be the most prosperous Villa for its growth of cattle and abundance of grain, because of its great fertility and for my having given it the spiritual and temporal patrons that I have chosen: namely, the ever glorious Apostle of the Indies, San Francisco Xavier, and Your Excellency, with whose names the town has been entitled Villa de Alburquerque de San Francisco Xavier del Bosque." Clearly the governor was bucking for favor when he gave the viceroy's name to the new town.

In conclusion, Cuervo declared, "The Villa was sworn, taking into account the things ordered by his Majesty in his royal laws." By the word "sworn" he meant that the heads of households had taken an oath as charter citizens to live upon and improve lands allotted to them as a requirement for gaining final title of possession.

From the foregoing statements, it is clear that Governor Cuervo intended to show that, through his own efforts, he had assembled a respectable number of colonists and chartered the new villa of Albuquerque; that he had ordered delineation of the outer boundaries of the community as well as the marking of a site for a plaza; and that he had caused a church and government offices to be built. Unfortunately, other evidence indicates that the ambitious governor, in his claims, strayed several degrees from the truth. Indeed, as a subsequent review of other documents will show, he uttered numerous half-truths and several outright falsehoods. Some doubt is, therefore, cast upon the traditional belief that Albuquerque was founded as a lawful Spanish municipality.

The subject is of more than academic interest. As child and

heir of the Spanish colonial villa, the modern city of Albuquerque has on occasion asserted claim to land and water rights in the courts by reference to Hispanic law governing the community at its founding. Such a stand has always been predicated upon the position that Governor Cuervo, true to his word to the king and viceroy, conducted the formal proceedings and followed the steps as stipulated by the *Recopilación* that were needed to establish Albuquerque as a legal entity.

In 1881 at the beginning of the boom occasioned by arrival of the railroad, the city of Albuquerque placed a petition before the state surveyor general asking that he survey a tract of four square leagues (roughly 17.2 square miles), centering upon the Old Town plaza, and then recommend to Congress that it place Albuquerque in possession. The claim was based upon a mistaken belief that old Spanish practice automatically granted four square leagues to each new villa. Although Governor Cuervo had never referred in existing documents to such a grant, attorneys for the city hoped to show that one had, indeed, been made.

The surveyor general of New Mexico evidently assumed as much, for he acted favorably upon Albuquerque's petition, surveyed the "imagined" four square leagues, and recommended it for confirmation by Congress. He was careful to explain to Washington, however, that "No original documents constituting or creating the grant hereby are known to exist, and therefore no such document can be filed herewith." What he supposed, as have most lawyers and historians since, was that the original grant papers, which Cuervo must have drawn up, had become lost over the years, but that unfortunate circumstance notwithstanding, Albuquerque was still entitled to its original allotment of land. The tough-minded congressmen, though, were not swayed by such an argument, and eventually the city's claim was disallowed.

The issue came up again in 1959, but this time in relation to water rights. The city became involved in a dispute with the state over use of waters in the surrounding Rio Grande Basin. It claimed that under Spanish law the villa of Albuquerque was conceded all the water necessary for its growth and development and that since the modern city was the legal heir of the villa, its right in this regard remained unimpaired. The New Mexico Supreme Court finally decided against the city on the basis of other legal points. Yet what is significant here is that much of Albuquerque's stand rested upon the popular assumption that in the year 1706 Governor Francisco Cuervo y Valdés officially established a valid community according to the laws of Spain.

It is now possible to clarify, in some measure, the incidents attendant upon Albuquerque's beginnings, particularly the actions of Governor Cuervo. But since serious gaps still exist in the documentary record, our picture, though revised and brought into sharper focus, remains disappointingly fuzzy around the edges. Keeping that fact in mind, we can begin by taking a close look at what was going on in New Mexico, and especially in the Middle Rio Grande Valley, during the years immediately before 1706.

When Governor Diego de Vargas died at Bernalillo in April 1704, his second-in-command, Juan Páez Hurtado, a native of Andalucia and a staunch soldier, took charge of the province. At once he notified the viceroy, the Duke of Alburquerque, of

Vargas's passing and then he set about holding things together until a replacement could be named.

Páez Hurtado had no easy task, for New Mexico was in a state of extraordinary disarray. Predatory bands of Apaches and Navajos stalked the small Spanish settlements and ranches, and nothing a few soldiers were able to do seemed to stem their constant attacks. Those same soldiers, in whose hands defense of the frontier lay, suffered from lack of provisions, a shortage of horses, inadequate pay, and low morale. Compounding the Indian problem, some of the western Pueblos still refused to submit to Spanish rule. The Zuñis, after first pledging loyalty, had changed their minds and, abandoning their pueblo, fled to a neighboring mesa top where they remained until a Spanish priest talked them down in 1705. The Hopis, still farther west, continued defiant and, indeed, would persist as a thorn in the side of Spanish governors throughout the remainder of the colonial period.

The settler folk who had come with Vargas in 1693 and others who arrived in a thin but steady trickle in succeeding years had not fared well. Government support in the form of provisions and tools sustained them initially, while they commenced to rebuild the province, but such aid was drastically curtailed in 1698 when officials of the royal treasury in Mexico City arbitrarily decided that New Mexicans should have made enough headway by then to go it alone. The loss of material backing unluckily coincided with the beginning of a severe drought, which stretched without relief from 1698 to 1704. Streams evaporated, scorched pastureland was grazed over and became ankle-deep in dust. Crops withered and produced at harvest scarcely enough seed for the next planting. Livestock wasted away. And hunger became a grim specter stalking the colonists. The stars, it seemed, were aligned against them.

The miserable economic conditions led inevitably to social discord. Petty controversies split the populace into squabbling factions and produced so much poisoned air that many embittered persons threatened to pull stakes and return to El Paso.

It was this atmosphere of despair and gloom that Francisco Cuervo y Valdés found when he arrived at Santa Fe on March 10, 1705, to take over the reins of government. He had received his appointment to office directly from the viceroy, on condition that the king approve. But since such approval might be months in coming, owing to the slowness of transatlantic mail service, Cuervo had hastened on to New Mexico to begin at once putting affairs there in order. Until confirmed in office, he would be acting merely as the provisional governor. That temporary status perhaps explains his strenuous efforts to make a good showing during the first months after his arrival.

Cuervo was well fitted by background and experience to follow in the footsteps of the lamented Governor Vargas. Born in Santa María de Grado in the province of Asturias, northern Spain, his family was evidently of the nobility, for noble lineage was one of the requirements for membership in the military order of Santiago, to which Cuervo was elected some time after 1698.

He arrived in the New World in the year 1678 and proceeded to Sonora (which included much of present-day southern Arizona) where he took up duties as an infantry captain. Three years later, he became lieutenant governor of the province. Thereafter, he served in succession as the military governor of the provinces of Nuevo León and Coahuila, which lay immediately south of Texas. It was his skillful performance in the handling of those offices and his wide knowledge of frontier affairs that led the Duke of Alburquerque to name him to the governorship of New Mexico late in 1704.

Once in Santa Fe, Cuervo made a hasty survey of local conditions and discovered excellent grounds for apprehension. The depth of his dismay is evident in words he addressed to the king. "I have never seen so much want, misery, and backwardness in my life," he wrote to His Majesty. "I suspect this land was better off before the Spaniards came." Such a candid admission indicates that the new governor was something of a realist.

Since military defense was one of his prime concerns, Cuervo undertook a quick inspection of the one hundred regular troops attached to the Santa Fe presidio. Then he called for a general muster of the citizens' militia. Because of the constant danger from hostile Indians, all able-bodied men were enrolled in militia companies. Under orders of the governor, those from the towns of Santa Cruz de la Cañada and Bernalillo marched to the capital for a review and inspection. The Bernalillo contingent, the military records note, was led by three captains: Fernando de Chávez, Diego de Montoya, and Manuel Baca. All were destined to play a prominent role in the early history of Albuquerque.

With a coldly professional eye, Governor Cuervo tallied up his forces, both regular and volunteer, and determined that their number was far too small to defend his broad domain. He fired off a letter to Mexico City asking for reinforcements, but, as he may well have anticipated, the economy-minded viceroy simply pigeonholed the request. No more soldiers were to be forthcoming.

The governor's next move was to take the troops already quartered in Santa Fe and spread them out on the frontier. He hoped that by patrolling the danger zones with small squads, he could stop the Apaches and other tribes from running roughshod over the New Mexican settlements. To that end, temporary detachments were stationed at the pueblos of Santa Clara, Cochiti, Jemez, Laguna, Acoma, and Zuñi.

As part of a broad policy to gain cooperation of the Pueblo Indians, Cuervo toured their villages, spoke to the leaders in conciliatory terms, and obtained promises of aid in the continuing war against the Apaches. From those meetings, he drew a high opinion of the Pueblo people, referring to them as handsome in appearance and industrious by nature. The Indians, for their part, responded favorably to the governor's overtures. Indeed, they came to regard him as something of a savior, or so he tried to convince the king. By letter, Cuervo declared immodestly that Pueblo spokesmen who gathered at Santa Fe in January 1706 voluntarily composed a document urging that "don Francisco Cuervo y Valdés be continued and maintained in this administration for such time as is His Majesty's will. . . ."

The implication is plain. Worried over his pending confirmation, the governor had contrived an endorsement from the Indians in a bid to polish his image and win approval from the crown. Something of the same motive, in part, was behind Cuervo's move to create a new villa in the Bosque de Doña Luisa. Certainly, he exaggerated on paper the dimensions of the project and his own role in its initiation, as we shall see shortly.

Actually, interest in founding a villa somewhere in the

Middle Valley of the Rio Grande had existed long before Cuervo y Valdés assumed the governorship. The idea first surfaced in 1662 when Governor Diego de Peñalosa made an unsuccessful attempt to promote a town in that area. The matter came up again after the revolt and reconquest. The municipal council of Santa Fe in 1698 called upon the governor to establish a villa in the Rio Abajo, but once more, nothing was done.

While officialdom may have been guilty of heel-dragging with regard to organizing a formal villa, the same could not be said for individual Spanish colonists who were eager to develop the potentially rich agricultural lands of the Middle Valley. Some of them, as mentioned earlier, had peeled off from Vargas's returning column in 1693 and reoccupied portions of the valley, especially the Bernalillo district. During the next several years, Governor Vargas had made a number of land grants to persons who desired farms in the country between Alameda and the swamps of Mejía. One of those grants, issued in the summer of 1704, went to Luís García, who reclaimed the estate of his grandfather, former Lieutenant-governor Alonso García.

The pueblo of Alameda itself, which had been burned by the Spaniards in the aftermath of the Pueblo Revolt, remained untenanted until 1702 when missionaries gathered about fifty stray Tiwas and rebuilt the village. This population, however, was evidently too small to maintain a viable community and, six years later, the Indians moved downstream and joined Isleta Pueblo. That left the abundant and fertile farmland stretching south from Bernalillo available to Spanish citizens who might wish to apply for grants.

One nucleus of settlement, predating the founding of Albuquerque, was the village of Atrisco, located on the west bank of the river and facing the site of the future villa. At least by 1703, the place was recognized as a community even though in form it was no more than a collection of farms. Lacking any municipal organization, Atrisco was attached for administrative purposes first to Bernalillo and, after 1706, to Albuquerque. Throughout the remainder of the colonial period, the village was a satellite of its larger neighbor, and, in fact, was often spoken of as "Atrisco de Albuquerque."

One thing is clear then: a number of Spanish property holdings existed on both sides of the Rio Grande well before Governor Cuervo certified to the king and viceroy in the spring of 1706 that he had founded the villa of Albuquerque. But in spite of that start, there had been no great rush of settlers from elsewhere in New Mexico to claim a share of the plentiful cropland and pasture available in the region. The vulnerability of the valley to Indian attack offered the major stumbling block to expansion of settlement. That problem Cuervo hoped to alleviate by stationing the detachment of ten soldiers at the new villa. Their presence plainly proved to be a key factor in luring colonists to Albuquerque.

Information surrounding the actual formation of the villa, including the ceremonial taking of possession and distribution of lands to residents, is very thin. Most writers have tried to reconstruct a picture of the event by reference to procedures set forth in Spanish law and to ceremonies, described at a later date, for the founding of other New Mexico towns. There would seem to be justification for such guessing because Governor Cuervo, as noted, did give the king flat assurance that in establishing Albuquerque he had followed the laws as set down in the *Recopilación*.

In a remote area, such as New Mexico, however, some flexibility in application of the laws seems to have been permitted. General Vargas, for example, upon creating the villa of Santa Cruz in 1695, placed it under an appointed alcalde mayor, who also had the title of militia captain, rather than under the usual elective municipal council, or cabildo. As he pointed out, he gave the town "this style and form of government because of its being on the frontier." In addition, he specifically decreed that Santa Fe, the first villa of the province, should alone have the privilege of operating under a municipal council. The precedent established by that order, as well as Albuquerque's status as a frontier community, perhaps explain why Governor Cuervo in chartering his new villa in 1706 provided it with an alcalde mayor rather than a cabildo.

A native-born New Mexican, forty-six-year-old Captain Martín Hurtado, was the man Governor Cuervo selected to serve as the first alcalde mayor of the villa of Albuquerque, as well as the commander of the ten-man military squad to be garrisoned there. To Hurtado must go credit for partitioning lands among charter members of the villa, which he did during January 1706, and for conducting the founding ceremony on the following February 7. We would like to believe that the assembled populace gathered at the spot selected for a plaza, participated in the marking off of streets and town lots, and helped designate the sites for a church and soldiers' quarters. They would also have followed behind Captain Hurtado while the town's lawful boundaries were measured and marked. In conformity with ancient Spanish custom, they would have pulled up grass, thrown rocks in the air, and shouted, "Long live the king!", symbolic acts associated with the taking possession of new lands. Later, some of the colonists recorded that they had sworn an oath, which confirms that some kind of formal proceeding took place. But whether the boundaries were actually surveyed and whether plaza, streets, lots, and commons were marked is open to question.

Further uncertainty surrounds the actual number of charter citizens. The governor's own declaration that there were thirty-five families with 252 people had generally been accepted by scholars. But Juan Candelaria, recollecting seventy years after the fact, stated that the villa got its start when twelve families from Bernalillo moved to the site, accompanied by the soldier escort that Governor Cuervo had assigned to them.

A wholly different picture emerges from the records of an investigation into the governor's activities, conducted in 1712, long after he had left office and returned to Mexico. At that time the king's ministers, while reviewing documents in their archive, discovered discrepancies in some of the claims put forth by former governor Cuervo y Valdés of New Mexico. As a result, they prevailed upon the crown to issue a royal *cédula,* or decree, directing the current governor of the province, Juan Ignacio Flores Mogollón, to open an official inquiry. Specifically, they wanted to know whether Albuquerque had been legally founded and whether the charter families had numbered thirty-five, as Cuervo maintained. They also asked that his claims to having created another villa north of Santa Fe, called Santa María de Grado, and having refounded the abandoned pueblos of Galisteo and Pojoaque with displaced Indians be examined.

At Santa Fe, Governor Flores Mogollón, upon receiving

the king's cédula, appointed Vargas's old friend and subordinate, General Juan Páez Hurtado, to carry out the investigation. The general spent several months traveling about the province taking depositions from citizens, and his findings, particularly as they relate to the beginnings of Albuquerque, are most illuminating.

Opening the judicial inquiry at the villa of Albuquerque on October 21, 1712, Páez Hurtado summoned witnesses and received their testimony "under the sign of the cross," that is, under oath. Here is the statement of Pedro Acenzio López:

> *Question:* Was he one of the founding citizens of the villa which was settled by order of Don Francisco Cuervo?
>
> *López:* That was true. He had joined with his father, Pedro López, when the governor founded it.
>
> *Question:* How many persons were in his family?
>
> *López:* Five.
>
> *Question:* Did he know the total number of founding families?
>
> *López:* There were nineteen original families, plus the ten soldiers, with their women and children, who served as guard for the vicinity. The nineteen families at the time comprised 103 people, not counting dependents of the soldiers. Now they totaled 129 people.
>
> *Question:* Had the said Don Francisco Cuervo provided them any government aid *(ayuda de costa)* at the founding?
>
> *López:* He knew of none.

*Question:* Had the villa been established in proper form with streets and a plaza?

*López:* He and the other settlers had moved into the houses abandoned by the Spaniards in 1680, occupying the same estancias and farms. What was called the villa stretched for more than two and a half miles (one league) from the first house to the last.

*Question:* Were there now any families here beyond those settled by Don Francisco Cuervo?

*López:* Yes. Seven additional families with twenty-two people.

Pedro López then declared that he knew no more about the matter and was dismissed. A succession of other witnesses gave similar testimony, in each case verifying López's population figures. From their statements, a few supplementary details can be gleaned. For example, Captain Fernando Dúran y Chávez, long one of the leading men of the valley, was asked if Albuquerque had been lawfully formed with streets and a plaza, as His Majesty required. He responded that from the day of its founding, the villa had the same layout as it did then, with the residents living in homes built before 1680. They were scattered for a league from the first house of Baltasar Romero on the north (at modern Ranchos de Albuquerque) to the last house on the south, that of Pedro López (below Central Avenue). All of this area, he noted, was heavily wooded *(en mucha alameda)*. And, he reports that it was by the authority of Governor Cuervo that the prerevolt estancias and farms were allotted to the new citizenry.

From these declarations, it can be seen that the governor's

original account to the king and viceroy in 1706 varied rather widely from that of the witnesses interviewed by General Páez Hurtado. Not only that, the general learned in his continuing investigation that Cuervo had fraudulently claimed to have created a new villa above Santa Fe, naming it after his birthplace in Spain, Santa María de Grado. No such town, in fact, had been founded. Further, while the governor had actually resettled the pueblos of Galisteo and Pojoaque in the north, he grossly inflated the number of Indians involved. All this Páez Hurtado entered into the formal record of his inquiry.

As already indicated, Governor Cuervo y Valdés seemed to have been intent upon currying favor among his superiors. No doubt, it was that simple motive that led him to color the truth. To the Spanish mind, the founding of a villa carried immense prestige, and the governor beyond question wished to add that accolade to his name. An eighteenth-century friar-scholar, Silvestre Vélez de Escalante, who composed a history of early New Mexico, wrote with biting sarcasm that Governor Cuervo, "eager to accumulate merits, falsified his reports." It is difficult to disagree with that judgment.

But where does that leave us with regard to the status and early history of Albuquerque? Must all of Cuervo's utterances on its founding be dismissed, or did he mix truth with fiction? Is it possible to draw any satisfactory conclusions on the matter at this late date?

Assimilating all currently available information, this much seems evident. Governor Cuervo, in writing to his superiors, portrayed himself as the architect of the new and glorious villa of Albuquerque. He erroneously claimed a founding population of thirty-five families, when in fact there was little more than half that number. Perhaps the governor pumped up the figure so that it would surpass, by a comfortable margin, the minimum requirement of thirty families as specified in the *Recopilación*. Very few of the other stipulations pertaining to new villas seem to have been met. Whatever was done must have been performed in the most casual, haphazard manner. At the time of the judicial inquiry of 1712, none of the witnesses indicated that even the elementary task of designating a plaza and streets had been carried out. Nor did they make reference to the building of a church, although other contemporary documents affirm that one was in progress during the villa's first years. Certainly, Governor Cuervo's solemn assertion to the king in 1706 that a church was already completed must be viewed with skepticism.

What appears to have occurred is this: Upon learning that ten soldiers were to be stationed in the area, nineteen families migrated to the Albuquerque Valley, probably coming in piecemeal fashion, and upon arrival they were assigned individual land grants. Many of those, especially the twelve families Juan Candelaria mentions as coming from Bernalillo, were actually reclaiming properties that had belonged to their ancestors before the revolt of 1680. All households, so far as we can tell, received private grants of farm and ranch land. There is no evidence that any family was enrolled as a member of the community grant alleged to have been made to the villa of Albuquerque. As the settlers in 1712 made plain, Albuquerque was not the usual compact urban town one thought of in connection with the rank and title of a villa. Rather, it was a mere collection of farms spread along the Rio Grande. From all reports, this pattern of dispersal continued throughout much of the century.

General Pedro de Rivera, for instance, while on a military inspection tour of New Mexico in 1726, passed through Albuquerque and observed that the majority of its population, made up of Spaniards, mestizos, and mulattoes, lived on scattered farms. In 1754, Father Manuel Trigo, traveling upriver from Isleta, spoke of reaching the villa, "or I might say the site of the villa of Albuquerque, for the settlers, who inhabit it on Sunday, do not live there. They must stay on their farms to keep watch over their cornfields, which are planted at a very pretty place three leagues distant, called La Alameda." And finally, as late as 1776, another priest, Fray Francisco Domínguez, spoke of the villa itself as consisting of only twenty-four houses located near the mission. "The rest of what is called Albuquerque," he wrote, "extends upstream to the north, and all of it is a settlement of farms on the meadows of the river for the distance of a league." It bears mentioning that throughout the colonial years, New Mexico's other villas, Santa Fe and El Paso del Norte, and especially Santa Cruz de la Cañada, all showed similar characteristics of population dispersal and lack of genuine urbanism.

After a church was up and functioning, the Albuquerque citizenry evidently erected second homes, or "Sunday residences," on or near today's Old Town Plaza. Thereafter, for at least the first three-quarters of the eighteenth century, the community retained this loose and informal aspect. Only gradually in later years did a body of permanent residents take root around an emerging plaza. But notwithstanding its uncharacteristic and extralegal design, the town was known from 1706 onward as the Villa of Albuquerque, and no one appears to have challenged its right to use the prestigious title of "villa."

The reasons early Albuquerqueans fanned out to settle private grants rather than congregating around a plaza within the limits of a formal town grant are not hard to find. Irrigable land, restricted to a narrow strip along the river, stretched for several miles north of the villa. The farming folk, from a purely practical point of view, desired to live close to their fields both to save time, which would have been lost had they traveled daily from town, and to be on hand to guard their crops from thieves and predators. Also, with the houses widely scattered, each family could take advantage of the open rangeland nearby on the mesas flanking the valley. Simply put, the people saw more advantage in developing their own independent rural properties than in grouping together to form a standard Hispanic villa.

Self-serving Governor Cuervo covered the truth of the matter under flowery language and with sweeping claims about his strict adherence to the law, in his formal certification and in reports to Mexico City and Madrid. If nothing else, he had a flair for invention. But he also possessed a dash of cleverness, which lay behind his bid to gain the good will of the viceroy by naming the new villa in his honor. The governor's motive aside, the town was fortunate in acquiring a distinctive and illustrious name.

In Spain the town of Alburquerque (spelled with the extra "r") lies in the province of Badajoz, close to the Portuguese border. It contains an impressive walled castle, the traditional home of the Dukes of Alburquerque. Dating from Roman times, its original name was Albaquercus, which derives from the Latin *albus quercus*, meaning "white oak." The municipal coat of arms, even today, bears a single white oak on a crimson field.

In 1464, Henry IV, king of Castile and León, created the Dukedom of Alburquerque. The first duke was Beltrán de la Cueva, and from him the title has descended in an unbroken line to its current holder, Beltrán Alfonso Osorio y Díez. Of interest to our story is the tenth man in the chain, don Francisco Fernández de la Cuerva Enríquez, who served as viceroy of New Spain from 1701 to 1708. It was he whom Governor Cuervo y Valdés of New Mexico sought to flatter by gracing the new villa on the Rio Grande with the noble name.

By all accounts, Viceroy don Francisco Fernández proved an able and efficient administrator, a man known to be courtly and affable in manner. Soon after taking office in Mexico City, he shored up the coastal defenses of the viceroyalty as protection against pirates and the navies of rival colonial powers. When not busy with affairs of state, he and his wife entertained at their palace with lavish theatrical productions and splendid banquets. No doubt, upon receipt of Governor Cuervo's document of certification, attesting to the founding of the villa of Alburquerque, the viceroy experienced genuine pleasure at seeing his family name thus complimented. But the news of the governor's action presented at least two legal problems. Therefore, he referred the matter for resolution to an appointed junta, or advisory council, which met in July 1706.

One point considered by the junta was the name selected by Governor Cuervo for his new villa. It so happened that a royal decree had just been received in Mexico City ordering that the next villa established in the viceroyalty be named San Felipe in honor of Felipe V, to commemorate his recent coronation. The members of the council found a way to comply with the decree by recommending that the name of Governor

Cuervo's town be changed to San Felipe de Alburquerque, thereby honoring both the king and the viceroy.

It will be recalled that originally Governor Cuervo had declared Albuquerque's patron saint to be San Francisco Xavier. Perhaps that was another ploy of his to please the viceroy, whose given name was also Francisco. But it is possible, too, that the governor was thinking of himself: his own name was Francisco, and his personal saint, San Francisco Xavier, as suggested by the fact that he christened one of his sons, Francisco Antonio Xavier y Cuervo. Then, there is still a third reason why this saint was a logical choice as the patron of Albuquerque. He had earlier been the patron of the household of don Francisco Trujillo (husband of Doña Luisa), whose home, before being sacked by the rebellious Pueblos in 1680, lay on or near the future site of the villa. As mentioned, one of the several popular names for the adjacent cottonwood grove was the Bosque Grande de San Xavier. Therefore, among the settler folk, the locality in 1706 was already strongly identified with that particular saint.

Be that as it may, the viceroy's advisors decided in favor of San Felipe. But they neglected to state whether the name now to be linked to the villa of Albuquerque referred to San Felipe Apostol, one of the Twelve Apostles, or to San Felipe Neri, a sixteenth-century Italian saint. Confusion over this omission lasted for many years. Since the matter was cloudy anyway, the people of Albuquerque and their priests did as they pleased and called their church San Francisco Xavier. At least that is what Fray Francisco Domínguez discovered when he arrived in 1776 to conduct an official ecclesiastical inspection. He found that a painting of San Francisco Xavier, as principal patron, occupied a prominent place over the main altar. Rummaging about in the storerooms of the church or friary, he turned up a tattered oil canvas of San Felipe Neri and ordered that it be installed over the altar, to replace the image of San Francisco Xavier. From that time forward, Albuquerqueans recognized San Felipe Neri as the town's official patron.

The viceregal junta in the summer of 1706 also took up a request submitted by Governor Cuervo that a bell, vestments, chalice, and other altar furnishings be sent to equip Albuquerque's first church. Since the law provided that such things should be given by the government, the advisors approved and authorized appropriate expenditures.

They were not so generous, however, when it came to the procedures Cuervo had followed in founding Albuquerque. In their report to the viceroy, they pronounced the governor wrong for establishing the villa without consulting Mexico City. But inasmuch as the town was already up and growing, the members judged that, for the general welfare of the realm, it could be permitted to continue. To avoid a similar misstep in the future, they ruled that the governor of New Mexico should refrain from establishing any more settlements unless he informed the viceroy in advance. That order was to be recorded in the archives of the villa of Santa Fe.

The Duke of Alburquerque, in accord with the conclusions of his junta, dispatched a lengthy mandate to Governor Cuervo, dated July 30, 1706, advising him of the foregoing rulings. He also included an unhappy piece of news. Shortly before the mail reached Spain bringing word that the viceroy had appointed Cuervo provisional governor of New Mexico and recommending that his position be made permanent, the king had given the job to someone else. Rather, he had sold the office to a wealthy admiral, Don Joseph Chacón, who was the Marqués de la Peñuela. This was not an uncommon practice. Whenever the crown was short of cash, it simply sold an overseas post to the highest bidder. Governor Cuervo, who had come up the hard way through long service on the frontier, was left out in the cold.

After waiting some months for his successor to arrive, Cuervo packed up his trunks and departed for Mexico City, late in 1707. As he passed downriver, through his scattered villa of Albuquerque, he must have been low in spirit. Sadly, there was no way he could peer into the future and perceive the legacy he was leaving behind: the small, badly formed town whose founding he had authorized and upon which he had bestowed the name Albuquerque was destined to flower one day into a great city.

# 3

# *Years of Struggle*

ALBUQUERQUE, DURING THE first century after its founding, witnessed sporadic episodes of high drama: Indian
attacks and reprisals, violent quarrels among the colonists,
famines, and plagues. But behind such troubles flowed the
quiet, unsensational stream of ongoing daily life that char-
acterized all New Mexican communities in the days of
Spain's colonial rule.

A traveler from Mexico coming up the Camino Real
for the first time, say in the decade of the 1790s, and
pausing for a day to stroll through Albuquerque's plaza
and along the wobbly, ill-defined streets would have
been struck by the mellow atmosphere of somnolence
and by a prevailing sense of timelessness. It was a place
where every phase of work and leisure was governed by
age-old custom, and where major events in man's life

cycle—birth, marriage, and death—were attended by cere-monies encrusted with tradition.

The citizens of Albuquerque, as our traveler might have seen, walked to their tasks in full sunlight, thinking their own thoughts, swayed by their own emotions, and wholly uncon-scious of being a part of the great tide of history. They were not cardboard men and women, flat and bloodless, existing in a dim twilight, as we often in our imagination tend to see people out of history. They were alive with purposes and desires of which we have only a small inkling.

The dusty, sunburned Albuquerque seen by our Mexican visitor was composed of a jumble of squat mud houses, neither stylish nor comfortable; an earth-walled church, whose cavern-ous interior held a funereal silence and a musty odor of antiq-uity that all adobe structures seem to acquire the day after they are built; and, to the west of the church, a cluster of barracks for the soldiers, which local citizens had graced with the title of El Presidio, though it was not really a fort.

These dun-colored buildings in the bright glare of midday seemed poor and humble. But when evening's last burst of sunlight shot a fan of long red streamers from the dark edge of the West Mesa, their walls grew rosy and from a distance the glow gave Albuquerque the aspect of a rich and wonder-ful town.

Ambling about the plaza, upon which faced the church and several of the most important residences, the traveler absorbed the sights and sounds and smells of colonial life, all merging to form a pleasing medley of impressions. Pure, untainted air, laced with the faint fragrance of juniper smoke from cooking fires, assailed the nostrils. From the distance came the sound of bleating goats, the wheezing, protesting bray of a burro, and the rhythmic thunk, thunk of an ax biting into sticks of firewood. On all sides could be heard the bubbling noises of children at play and the occasional yowling of an infant. From neighboring houses issued the rasping sound of women grinding corn on stone metates and the bump and clack of weavers at work on heavy Spanish looms. Each of these sounds, together with the hollow ring of the church bell at noontide, was clear and distinct. They punctuated the heavy silence that enveloped all the land—the silence that has become one of our lost and now unremembered luxuries.

The people one saw, passing through Albuquerque's early-day plaza, formed a cross-section of the Rio Abajo population. There were big-hatted ranchers, with silver buttons on their clothing and a bright sash at the waist, who were mounted on small and wiry horses. Men of more humble station walked, carrying crude farm implements on their shoulders. They dressed in loose-fitting shirts and trousers made of *sabanilla*, a rough white cloth produced locally. Or sometimes they wore *gamuza*, the tanned skin of deer and elk as soft to the touch as velvet. Younger women, lithe and shapely, decked themselves out in blouse and skirt, and like the men shod their feet with *teguas*, the hard-soled moccasin used everywhere in New Mexico. Matronly ladies of advanced years, their faces lined and gullied by time and the weather, were usually attired in conservative black with a fringed *tápalo*, or shawl, wrapped around the head hood-fashion. Small children ran naked and were quickly tinctured nut-brown by the sun.

Leaving the plaza and moving up the valley on the Camino Real, our visitor from Mexico would have encountered the patchwork of farms that helped feed the villa of Albuquerque. Upon the fields, the Rio Grande's seasonal floods deposited a layer of fine alluvial soil. One New Mexican in 1773 remarked graphically that, "The water brings with it a thick mud which serves as manure for the land, leaving on top of the irrigated earth a glutinous scum resembling lard." The plots, thus fertilized, yielded bountiful crops of corn and wheat, vegetables like chile, squash, beans, and onions, and, of course, *punche,* the brown and acrid native tobacco smoked by everyone in little flat cornhusk cigarettes. In addition, one could find wondrously green vineyards that grew grape-heavy in late summer, and orchards of peach, apricot, plum, and apple.

A veritable net of *acequias,* or irrigation ditches, allowed the fields to drink between rains. Where they crossed the Camino Real and smaller feeder roads, the acequias were spanned by clumsy log bridges. The main ditch, the *acequia madre,* siphoned off water from the Rio Grande several miles above the villa, then ran along the eastern edge of the valley, near the foot of the tumbled sandhills. From it, tributary ditches dropped down to the individual fields where farmers, using wide-bladed hoes, caused the water to spread evenly over the thirsty soil. The ditch system had been started by the pre-Revolt settlers, and it had been restored and expanded by the tillers who reclaimed the valley in 1706. At the gurgling acequias, Albuquerque's populace drew water for drinking, and in them they bathed, washed their clothes, and watered livestock. Beyond such purely practical functions, the ditches, sparkling under the sun and shining like yellow ribbons by moonlight, lent much to the pastoral beauty of the countryside north of the villa.

Journeying up the Camino Real, following the deep ruts cut by cart caravans, the wayfarer passed a succession of ranchos, the small farmsteads with a two- or three-room adobe house, an outdoor beehive oven, and out back a few sheep and burros quartered in tight little pens of juniper pickets (coyote fences, they are still called). Occasionally larger establishments could be seen: the multiroomed houses with a portal and tiny chapel belonging to aristocratic families who set their tables with a few treasured pieces of silver and were waited upon by Indian servants captured from the Apaches or Navajos.

This was the small, close-knit, almost self-sufficient Albuquerque of two centuries ago. The villa, its neighboring farms, and the way of life seen by our Mexican visitor have been swallowed up by the past, all but a few traces and faint echoes of that earlier time buried under the bustling hubbub of today's sprawling city. Yet, among the faded and fragile colonial documents, carefully preserved in public archives, can be found a record, spotty and incomplete though it is, of history's high points during those years when the Spanish flag floated over the Albuquerque plaza.

Most abundant in the old papers are references to Indian raids that kept the Middle Valley in constant turmoil far into the nineteenth century. Governor Vargas's last illness in 1704 had overtaken him while pursuing Apaches through the Sandia Mountains, and although none of his successors fared so badly as to die on a campaign, they all had to devote a considerable portion of their time to keeping the hostile tribes in check.

During his brief administration, Governor Cuervo y Valdés prosecuted the war "with all vigor," as he put it. He mounted two campaigns against the Navajos on the west, and three against the Apaches of the south and east. His military efforts met with some success, for as he wrote to the Duke of Alburquerque in mid-1706, "By these operations, the kingdom has attained the quiet, peace, and tranquility which it now enjoys."

In the interval of calm, which is all it proved to be, an Apache arrived in Albuquerque and spoke to the alcalde mayor, Captain Martín Hurtado. He said that members of his band camping in the Sandias had a vision in which they were encouraged to accept Spanish authority and to trade with the people of the new villa. It was an obvious and disarming ploy on the part of the Apaches to gain a breathing spell from the constant harassment they had lately suffered at the hands of the governor's forces. But it was also an expression of their desire to engage in honest trade—that being an acceptable alternative when the preferable business of raiding proved too risky.

Captain Hurtado doubtless put little stock in the "vision" claimed by the Indians, but he was warm to their proposal for opening commerce. Shortly, he notified Governor Cuervo of "the peaceful visits made by the pagans of the Apache nation," and described their repeated trips "to barter with the Spanish inhabitants of the villa of Albuquerque and with the Christian Pueblos . . . of this district and jurisdiction." The colonists, whose markets were extremely limited, eagerly sought traffic with the nomadic Indians, knowing full well that the tribesmen had stolen from them in the past and would for a certainty steal from them again in the future. The arrangement—alternating war with trade—became an established practice on the New Mexican frontier.

On numerous occasions, the Hispanic settlers, not content to wait for the Indians to come to them, carried mule loads of merchandise into the wilds looking for customers. The royal governors ineffectually attempted to regulate such commerce by requiring traders to get licenses. Governor Juan Ignacio Flores Mogollón, for example, issued an order in 1712 providing that persons caught at illegal trading would be jailed for four months, and that alcaldes mayores who winked at such activities in their districts would be removed from office and given a two-month jail term. The stern order was proclaimed by town criers in Albuquerque, Bernalillo, and other communities in the province. But no one paid it much attention.

The peace Governor Cuervo had won in 1706 lasted barely a year. About the time he was transferring the reins of government to his successor, the Marqués de Peñuela, late in 1707, Apaches and Navajos resumed attacks upon Albuquerque's Middle Valley with all their old ferocity. At the end of the year, a war party of Apaches seized one hundred head of cattle belonging to residents of the villa and disappeared toward the southwest. Martín Hurtado got a hurried message off to Santa Fe asking for help, and Captain Félix Martínez, commander of the Santa Fe presidio, responded promptly. With thirty crack troops and sixty Pueblo militiamen, he arrived in Albuquerque where he enlisted a number of local settlers to give his punitive force still more muscle. Then he went pelting off on the trail of the thieves. He surprised them in their lair, situated in the Ladron Mountains thirty-five miles below Albuquerque, and delivered a knockout punch. His men killed some of the warriors and scattered the rest of the band. Such chases were repeated innumerable times in the years following, but only rarely did the Spaniards earn a clear victory as they had on this occasion.

The Albuquerque folk experienced added raids in 1708, and their losses they blamed on the Marqués de Peñuela. Soon after taking office, the new governor had called in the small squads of soldiers that had been stationed around the province, believing that it was better to have the Santa Fe garrison at full strength. Incensed at losing the ten-man guard given them by Governor Cuervo, residents of Albuquerque authorized two of their leading spokesmen, Fernando Durán y Chávez and Baltazar Romero, to petition for redress.

In a formal document sent to Peñuela, the petitioners declared, in part, "The governor has been pleased to take away our squad, for which reasons, the enemy, seeing our weakness, has dared commit barbarous robberies, daily running off stock from our corrals. And now, knowing they will not be punished, they may be planning to surprise and destroy us and our wives and children. Before, they did not venture such an attack because of the presence of the soldiers. So for these reasons, we pray that the governor will be pleased to grant the return of our squad." After some indecision and delay on the part of Peñuela, the Albuquerqueans, much to their relief, got back their contingent of troops.

The people's fear of the Apaches and Navajos, when the tribes were in a warring mood, was fully justified. On June 8, 1709, an enormous army of Navajos fell upon Jemez Pueblo northwest of Albuquerque, sacked the small government building and church, and made away with the priests' vestments and sacred vessels from the altar. Two squads of soldiers went in pursuit. In a running fight, they killed a few warriors and wounded others, but, owing to the large numbers of the enemy, failed to inflict a decisive defeat. The very next month, Navajos struck again at Santa Clara Pueblo north of Santa Fe. In retaliation, Governor Peñuela summoned the provincial militia (including, presumably, citizens of Albuquerque), and sent it with a strong body of regular troops on a major sweep through western New Mexico. The campaign chalked up several major victories, and as a result the Navajos sued for peace, which as expected, proved only temporary.

The Apaches, bellicose as ever, continued to plague the New Mexicans. Members of the Faraon band haunted the Sandias, seizing every opportunity to cause mischief among settlers in the Middle Valley. In 1714, Juan Ignacio Flores Mogollón, who had succeeded Peñuela as governor, mounted a major expedition against them, composed of 36 soldiers, 11 residents of Albuquerque, and 321 Pueblo auxiliaries drawn from villages as far north as Taos. This force, bristling with weapons, followed the trail of the Faraon Apaches who had stolen some cattle in the vicinity of Bernalillo. The Spaniards with their Pueblo allies marched through the Cañada de Carnué, scouted the mountains, and came up empty-handed. Time after time, the story was repeated. The Indians, knowing the country and the best escape routes, would make a lightning raid, and then skip away, staying two jumps ahead of their pursuers.

As the leading community in the Rio Abajo, Albuquerque became a main assembly point for campaigns launched against hostile Indians in the lower half of the province. Its open square facing the church was designated a *plaza de armas,* a parade ground where troops could be mustered and stand in review. Military operations occurred with such frequency that people of the villa came to regard the clank of arms and the rattle of drums as a familiar, if unwished for, part of life. Like families everywhere in time of war, women and children must have gathered solemn-faced at the edge of the plaza each time their menfolk mounted up and rode off to do battle. They would have made an impressive sight, those citizen volunteers of Albuquerque. Each reported for duty bearing his own weapons, wearing a padded leather vest meant to fend off arrows, and leading extra horses and mules, which would be needed on forced marches. Those of substantial means brought along a personal servant to wait on them along the trail and to do double-duty as a soldier in case of a fight.

Although the Albuquerqueans willingly responded when called by the governor to take the field, they seem to have been downright negligent when it came to defending their immediate locale. At least that was the opinion of Governor Tomás Vélez Cachupín, who took office in 1749 for a five-year term. "The settlers of Albuquerque," he remarked acidly, "wish to have a soldier for every cow and horse they pasture so that they would have nothing to worry about and could live in slovenly indifference. I have tried to accustom them to the idea that each one should take care of the defense of his own hacienda. The number of settlers in that area is sufficient to do so. Besides, they are well trained and experienced in war."

The fact was, the residents of the villa were so spread out and their livestock was allowed to graze so far on the mesas that they were vulnerable to any stray war party looking for easy pickings. They received an upbraiding from Vélez Cachupín's successor, Governor Francisco Marín del Valle, who issued a formal order calling attention to the carelessness shown by the people of Albuquerque in the guarding of their animals. Often, he said, they just turned the horse herds loose to forage, leaving them prey for the Indians. The governor threatened to fine and jail anybody guilty of such irresponsibility.

But the Indian troubles endured by the valley colonists in the first half of the eighteenth century paled when stacked against what followed. A new and more deadly foe, the Comanche, appeared out of the north, unleashing frightful assaults all along the Spanish frontier. For three decades after 1750 the New Mexicans suffered a series of maulings, and not through any failure of nerve on their part. The settlers were peppery enough. As Governor Vélez Cachupín had suggested of the Albuquerqueans, they were trained and knew how to hold up their end in a scrap.

The problem lay with the Comanches themselves. Unlike the Apache and Navajo, who usually came by stealth in small bands and were content to grab a flock of sheep and maybe a captive or two, then break for the hills, the Comanches rode in massive parties of several hundred and ravaged the entire countryside. Woe to anyone who tried to follow them when their bloody work was done, for they were masters at maneuvering in the open and at laying deadly ambushes. That became gruesomely apparent when a befeathered Comanche host devastated the Middle Valley between Sandia and Alameda in June of 1775. Walled Sandia Pueblo easily repelled the invaders, but as they departed, the Comanches drove off virtually every horse, cow, and sheep belonging to the village. Unstrung by the crippling loss, thirty-three Pueblo men improvidently set off on foot after the attackers. The Comanches at first feigned retreat. But as the Pueblos became exhausted by their running, the

Comanche warriors turned and slew them to a man. Afterward, they wantonly butchered the slow-moving cattle and sheep and then disappeared with the captured horses. The episode left little Sandia Pueblo benumbed, and increased the fear already stalking neighboring Albuquerque, Bernalillo, and the other Spanish communities.

The Pueblo Indians, as long as they stayed in their fortress-like villages, were safe enough, but the colonists, dispersed on their farms, were as exposed as always. A keen-eyed priest, Father Damián Martínez, charged that, "Every compact pueblo, even those with a small population, is capable of mounting a vigorous defense. This can be seen at the pueblo of Sandia, which has the smallest number of fighting men. The strongest of our enemies, the Comanches, dare not attack it, but instead raid Albuquerque with impunity because the population there, although more numerous, is badly scattered."

In the teeth of the Comanche threat, New Mexico's governors regularly issued proclamations encouraging the beleaguered people to abandon their dispersed farmsteads and unite in defensible towns. From the government's viewpoint, such a course was eminently practical because it meant the citizens themselves could shoulder most of the responsibility for repelling the war-hungry Comanches. Farmers and ranchers, loath to leave their property unattended, would have preferred to see an increase in soldiers and an expansion of military patrols, with the added expense footed by the royal treasury. That attitude explains penny-pinching Governor Vélez Cachupín's earlier complaint that "the settlers of Albuquerque wish to have a soldier for every cow and horse they pasture." When it became manifestly clear that such was not to be, many of the rural folk, under the spur of Comanche pressure, began to move into compact settlements. Spanish colonists in the Taos Valley, which was extraordinarily accessible to invasion, left their far-flung homes and took up quarters behind the walls and towers surrounding Taos Pueblo. On the frontier east and west of the Rio Grande, some hamlets regrouped and built fortified quadrangles with homes around the perimeter facing inward on an enclosed plaza.

At Albuquerque, there is no evidence of the building of any walls, bastions, or other military defenses during this troublous period. But there does seem to have been some shift of population from outlying areas to the inner precincts of the villa. Father Domínguez, as already quoted, could observe no more than twenty-four houses in the center of Albuquerque as late as 1776, but even that represented significant urban clustering when compared to the straggled condition of the villa in earlier decades.

There was not the slightest doubt in the mid-1770s that the Rio Grande Valley was caught in a deadly bear hug, with the Comanches of the north applying pressure on one side and the Apaches and Navajos doing the same from the opposite direction. On June 18, 1774, two hundred Comanches hit Albuquerque, killing two Spaniards and three friendly Indians, abducting four sheepherders, and stealing the villa's horse herd. The offenders made an easy escape because the militia was absent at the time campaigning against the Navajos. The following summer Apaches pillaged the country below the villa, leaving fifteen dead. At the village of Valencia, also downstream, twenty-three lost their lives in a Comanche incursion of May 1777. On August 27, ten Albuquerque men and a woman were massacred in still another blood bath. The galling casualties produced by such onslaughts made many people wonder if the colony could survive.

Happily for New Mexico, a savior arrived in the person of Don Juan Bautista de Anza, who assumed the governorship in 1778. A seasoned Indian fighter with previous experience in Sonora and California, Anza knew what he was about. A serious face, highlighted by a prominent nose, broad forehead, and pointy chinbeard gave him the appearance of a philosopher. But the peaceful exterior belied the stern, unyielding qualities of the inner man. When he observed the New Mexicans, worn to a frazzle, and perceived the disastrous state of the local economy, reduced to near ruin by continuous Indian warfare, he acted with decision and dispatch.

First, he inspired and reorganized available provincial forces—the regular troops, citizen volunteers, and Pueblo auxiliaries. Then, by careful deployment and adroit maneuvering, he managed to blunt the worst inroads of the Indian foe. Concentrating on the Comanche threat, the governor within a year brought about a drastic curtailment of their raids, allowing the settlers and Pueblo Indians a much overdue respite from terror.

For the tenacious Anza, however, that was only the beginning. In hopes of achieving a permanent solution, he decided to carry the fight into the home country of the Comanches. In late 1779, he mustered an army of six hundred men, led it over the Rockies to the main Indian camps in eastern Colorado, and administered the enemy a resounding defeat. His action broke the back of Comanche resistance and paved the way, a few years later, for a general peace with the entire tribe.

During the 1780s, Albuquerque commenced a slow recovery. Apaches still committed petty raids on occasion, but with the Comanche threat lifted, the men of the villa cooperating with the king's soldiers were able to establish a measure of security that had heretofore been entirely lacking. The welcome calm, relative though it may have been, encouraged the birth of new settlements in the Middle Valley and allowed others, which had been started earlier but withered owing to Indian hostilities, to gain a new lease on life. A brief look at these small satellite communities of Albuquerque will be useful for achieving a better understanding of the history of the villa in later colonial times.

First, though, mention must be made of the troubled story of the Tiwa Pueblos. Their once thriving and populous province of Tiguex had, by the end of the seventeenth century, been thoroughly demolished by the shattering upheavals of the Pueblo Revolt and reconquest. In 1700, not a single Tiwa village remained in the Middle Valley. Many of the original inhabitants survived, however, and lived as refugees among other pueblos around the province. The largest body of Tiwas had fled west to the Hopis during Vargas's reconquest, and there built a pueblo called Payupki on Second Mesa.

The Spaniards felt some remorse over the fate of these dispossessed people, and, in 1702, they made the first of several attempts to reestablish the Tiwas along the Middle Rio Grande. In that year, as we have previously noted, Alameda was refounded near its original site with about fifty Indians. Father Juan de Zabaleta, minister at Bernalillo, directed the project and saw to the building of a tiny church dedicated to San Joseph. Later the population was swelled by the arrival of a handful of Tiwas from Hopi, but even so the pueblo was too small to ward off Apache attacks. Hence, in 1708 or 1709, the whole endeavor was given up and the people joined Isleta Pueblo downriver, which was in the process of reforming.

Lands abandoned by the Alameda Tiwas soon attracted the attention of Spanish settlers. In 1710, Governor Peñuela made a large grant, which became known as the Alameda tract, to Captain Francisco Montes Vigil as a reward for military service. Two years later the captain sold the grant to Juan González, who built a small chapel, containing a belfry, in honor of Our Lady of the Conception. Smaller parcels of land were given to other families, mainly from Albuquerque, for the development of ranchos. From these beginnings, the hamlet of Alameda soon emerged. Its nucleus was the house and chapel of the González family. In 1744, the community contained only eight families, but by the 1770s, it had grown to sixty-six families with 388 persons.

At the ruins of Isleta Pueblo south of Albuquerque, the Spaniards made their second attempt to congregate the displaced Tiwas. It will be recalled that back in 1681, Governor Antonio de Otermín, upon failing to retake New Mexico from the rebellious Pueblos, had burned Isleta and marched 385 of its people south to El Paso. There the captives had been installed in a new community, Isleta del Sur. Father Juan de la Peña was serving as their priest when, in May 1708, the Franciscan Order selected him to be chief prelate, or head, of all the New Mexico missions. Traveling upriver to assume his new duties, Father Peña conceived the idea of repopulating old Isleta. By late 1708 or early 1709, he was able to collect a fair number of Tiwas, including the residents of Alameda, refugees scattered among other Rio Grande Pueblos and among the Apaches, and some of the people who had been living with the Hopis. It is quite possible, too, that a few members of his former parish at Isleta del Sur may also have moved up and joined in the new venture.

To launch the reborn pueblo of Isleta, Father Peña provided its founding residents with cattle and supplies and directed rebuilding of the old church, which he named San Agustín. The village was settled and fully functioning at least by the winter of 1709, for the first reference to an Apache raid on the place appears at that time. Peña seems to have initiated and carried out the refounding solely upon his authority as head of the provincial church. Governor Peñuela did not give his formal consent and offers of aid until January of 1710.

Isleta, unlike the pueblo of Alameda, survived and prospered. Its population, increasing slowly but steadily, reached 304 by 1760, and finally climbed to 1,000 in 1880. In the latter half of the colonial period, the pueblo served as a partial buffer between Albuquerque and the Apaches who roamed southern New Mexico. And the ample produce of its grain fields and vineyards contributed materially to the developing economy of the Middle Valley.

At Sandia, the Spaniards made one more try at resettling the Tiwas in their old homeland. The pueblo and its adjacent farms, lying between Albuquerque and Bernalillo, had remained vacant since the time of the great revolt. In 1733 a group of *genízaros* asked the governor for permission to occupy the deserted village. Genízaros comprised a class of Indians peculiar to New Mexico: they were people who as children had been purchased or captured from far-roaming nomadic tribes—Apache, Ute, Kiowa, Pawnee, and Wichita. Growing up in the New Mexican settlements, they became thoroughly Hispanicized, losing all traces of their former tribal identities and languages.

Properly speaking, they were bound servants, not slaves. Upon deaths of their masters, many genízaros were freed. At first they tended to take up residence with the Pueblos, but having abandoned most of their Indian ways, they were not happy there. Feeling a common kinship among themselves, they began petitioning the governor for lands to form their own communities. One of the first such requests was for the tract containing the ruins of Sandia Pueblo. In this instance, the governor, Don Gervasio Cruzat y Góngora, denied their petition, but a few years later, in 1740, the genízaros were given land at Valencia, near Tomé Hill, a few miles south of Albuquerque.

The governor's reluctance to regrant the Sandia tract no doubt reflected his hope that some of its original Tiwa occupants could one day be collected and induced to rebuild the old village. That hope, in fact, was fulfilled in the following decade through the efforts of a pair of Franciscan missionaries.

In September of 1742, Father Pedro Ignacio Pino, resident priest at Albuquerque, and Father Carlos Delgado, missionary to the Isletas, journeyed westward to the land of the Hopi villages. The Indians there, independent since 1680, had repeatedly rebuffed attempts by the Spaniards to bring them back into the fold of the Church. What was more, they offered refuge to Rio Grande people like the Tiwas who had fled rather than accept Spanish rule. The two padres intended to try again to convert the Hopis and to lure back the dislocated Tiwas. Unexpectedly, they met with some success.

At Payupki, the new Tiwa village built, like its Hopi neighbors, high on a mesa top, Pino and Delgado discovered that a majority of the Indians were longing for their old homes and were willing to return with the friars. Moreover, a group of Hopis, who had recently been ousted from their village of Oraibi in a factional dispute, also asked to go. Although some of the very old and very young could not be taken, because of the lack of riding animals, a total of 441 people accompanied the missionaries back to the New Mexican settlements.

It was the intention of Fathers Pino and Delgado to install the new arrivals at a site near Albuquerque, preferably Sandia. But the then governor, Gaspar Domingo de Mendoza, refused to allow it, saying that permission would have to be obtained from the viceroy. In the meantime, the footsore refugees were given temporary shelter at Jemez and other pueblos.

Six years passed before the required license was obtained from Mexico City, but at last in 1748 it came, and the governor issued a decree providing for the reestablishment of the pueblo of Sandia. In May the lieutenant-governor, Don Bernardo de Bustamante Tagle, went to the site and placed the Indians in possession, distributing lands, waters, and pastures, and marking the corners of the grant with stone monuments surmounted by a wooden cross. He also announced that the pueblo would be under the administrative jurisdiction of the alcalde of Albuquerque. Several Spaniards, who were landowners on the west side of the Rio Grande opposite Sandia, appeared before him, worried that the new pueblo might encroach on their property. Bustamante explained to these men that the law allowed the Indians to have a league (2.6 miles) in each direction from their village. But he said that on the west he would measure only as far as the river, and since that distance was not a full league, he would compensate the Indians by a larger measurement to the east. In consideration of this, however, the Spaniards would have to agree to allow the Sandia people to graze stock on their side of the river where it was safer from seizure by Apaches. To that proposal, they willingly assented.

Thus, Sandia got its new beginning and became Albuquerque's nearest Pueblo neighbor on the north. Of the seventy families making up its original population, the majority were Tiwa and the remainder Hopi. For many years, the two groups lived in separate and distinct precincts of the pueblo. By keeping slightly apart, each was able to maintain its own language and customs. But in the mid-1770s, with the Comanche war at its height, the governor at Santa Fe ordered the Hopis to move in with the Tiwas so as better to resist attack. With that, the Hopis were rapidly absorbed, although in the process they left a strong mark on Sandia's culture. Even today, each May 15 the pueblo performs kachina ceremonies in its plaza (to which white men are not admitted) that are strictly Hopi in origin.

Once the matter of the Tiwas was settled—Sandia being the last project of the Spaniards to reestablish them in the Middle Valley—colonists quickly filled in the few remaining areas of cropland available above and below Albuquerque. Between Sandia's southern boundary and the northern limits of the villa, a cluster of farms soon became recognized as the community of Ranchos de Albuquerque. Its lands had been granted initially to Captain Diego Montoya by Governor Peñuela back in 1712. Shortly afterward they were conveyed to Elena Gallegos, the widow of Santiago Gurulé. (As was often done in colonial New Mexico, she retook her maiden name upon her husband's death.) The property, which became known as the Elena Gallegos grant, amounted to an estimated seventy thousand acres, much of it on the East Mesa and in the Sandia Mountains. When she died in 1731, Elena asked in her will to be interred inside Albuquerque's parish church, "near the font of Holy Water," and requested that her burial be solemnized with a High Mass and wake. More to the point, she willed her estate to her only child, Antonio Gurulé. He lived on the grant, in a six-room house, until his own passing in 1761.

As the eighteenth century wore on, the descendents and heirs of Elena Gallegos and her son, Antonio, subdivided the irrigable bottomlands along the Rio Grande into long, narrow strips that ran from the river to the foot of the sandhills. Some of the strips were passed on to children of the next generation, while others were sold to outsiders. The greater portion of the grant, that part lying on the mesa and in the mountains, continued to be held and used in common. Anyone owning even the smallest particle of land within the grant was permitted to pasture his stock there.

The farms known as Ranchos de Albuquerque constituted only one of several little settlements that took root on the Elena Gallegos grant in later years. Most were populated, at the outset at least, by a single extended family that gave its name to the hamlet—such places as Los Griegos (just inside the southern boundary of the grant and hence closest to the villa of

Albuquerque), Los Montoyas, Los Poblanos, and Los Gallegos. The Spanish custom of naming communities after the leading resident family was widely followed in the Middle Valley, so that in addition to those just mentioned, one could encounter, moving south from Albuquerque, place-names like Los Barelas, Los Armijos, Los Padillas, Los Lunas, and Los Chávez.

One exception was Los Corrales, which, according to local tradition, took its name from the extensive corrals built on the west side of the Rio Grande by rancher Juan González, founder of Alameda. It was actually two communities: Santa Rosalía de Corrales, or Upper Corrales, opposite Sandia Pueblo; and San Ysidro de Corrales, or Lower Corrales, immediately to the south. Of the two, Lower Corrales was more prosperous, possessing wider fields and better grazing. Father Domínguez counted twenty-six families there in 1776, as compared to only ten families for Upper Corrales, which, he observed, had "not very good lands."

By 1750, Albuquerque and its satellite communities were beginning to feel the pressure of overpopulation. Many of the valley farms, divided and redivided through inheritance, were reduced to long strips stretching from the river to the acequia madre at the foot of the sandhills, a pattern necessary so that each piece of land bequeathed to a child would touch the main irrigation ditch. Moreover, growth of the livestock industry, which had proceeded apace in spite of the dents made by Indian marauders, was placing a heavy strain on nearby graze. Increasingly, sons of large families, finding their economic prospects dim in the Middle Valley, began to cast hopeful glances west, toward the Rio Puerco.

Among the earliest to pull stakes and migrate westward

were twelve men, most of whom were related to the villa's first families. They included five Montaño brothers, a Chávez, a Gallegos, a Baca, and a Candelaria. In petitioning the governor for a grant of land on the Rio Puerco, Bernabé Montaño acted as spokesman for the rest and filed the necessary papers because, as he explained it, "the others don't know how to sign their names."

In doleful terms, he informed the governor on October 21, 1753, how he and the remaining petitioners were being nudged out of their native Albuquerque because of diminished opportunities for making a living. The few lands they owned were not sufficient to sustain their families, and pasturage on the mesas was so thin, they feared the coming winter would see their weakened livestock perish. To make ends meet, some of their number had gone to work at pueblos close by, weeding the fields and hauling firewood from the mountains in return for a few ears of corn, which is all the Indians paid them.

Plainly, it rankled Bernabé Montaño and his companions to find themselves in such a demeaning and impoverished condition, though they may well have exaggerated their woes a bit to gain the sympathy of the governor. They reinforced the appeal with a reminder of their own merits and those of their forebears. "We are worthy of this concession," wrote Bernabé, "since our grandfathers and fathers served His Majesty in the conquest and reconquest of New Mexico, while we, all our adult lives, have aided the king by taking part in every campaign against enemy Indians to which we were called. All this service notwithstanding, up to this moment we have never asked the government for a single bit of land [*ni un pedazo de tierra*]."

These impassioned arguments could not have failed to stir the governor, Tomás Vélez Cachupín. We know anyway that later in the year he issued a large grant on the Rio Puerco to Montaño and the others and instructed them at the same time to erect a fortified settlement with a square plaza and a single gate as entrance, so that "the families might defend themselves from invasions by barbarous Apaches."

In December, normally the coldest month in New Mexico, the twelve Albuquerqueans rode to their grant, about twenty miles west of the villa, and there met the alcalde mayor of Jemez who was to conduct the appropriate legal ceremony. He dutifully inscribed in the official record: "And they all entered into possession thereof by plucking up weeds, scratching up the ground, casting stones, and shouting in loud voices, 'Long live the King and Sovereign Don Fernando VI,' and we all shouted simultaneously, 'Huza! Huza!'"

Upon their new town, located a short distance east of the Puerco, the settlers bestowed the name Nuestra Señora de la Luz, San Fernando y San Blas, though in common parlance it came to be simply San Fernando. By that title, the people obviously wished to honor the king for whom they had so warmly uttered their "Huzas."

Before many years elapsed, the San Fernando folk had a batch of unwelcome neighbors on the south. These later arrivals also originated in the Middle Valley, but they came from Atrisco rather than Albuquerque. Since the Rio Grande and the lands of the villa hemmed them in on the east, the Atrisqueños had been forced by necessity to expand their stock-raising activities toward the Puerco. As they spread farther and farther westward with their flocks and herds, across the desert grassland where Folsom men had once hunted the longhorn bison, they approached San Fernando and the boundary of what had come to be called the Bernabé Montaño grant. There they got a hostile reception, for the old settlers were not eager to share their large domain with the newcomers. In fact, they rudely chased them back to Atrisco.

In 1768 the Atrisqueños complained to the governor about the ill treatment they had received, and they asked for their own grazing grant south of the Bernabé Montaño grant. There was plenty of room along the Puerco for everybody, they contended—with considerable justification. And, beside, their presence would serve as a bulwark for the defense of both San Fernando and the Albuquerque area, since along the Puerco "barbarous Apaches," as well as Navajos, were as thick as thorns on a cactus. The governor saw the logic in this, and they got their grant.

The reference to the Indian danger was well founded. Indeed, the Puerco Valley settlers suffered such a volley of ferocious attacks, principally from the Navajo, that by 1774 practically all of them had been driven back to the Rio Grande. In subsequent years, the Spaniards reclaimed the area for short terms, but its continuing status as an exposed and perilous frontier zone discouraged any extensive settlement during the late colonial period.

The story was repeated, on a smaller scale, immediately east of Albuquerque. In 1762, some nineteen poor and landless inhabitants of the Middle Valley obtained a grant at the Cañon de Carnué. They planned to build homes there, grow crops, taking advantage of springs and a small stream in the bottom of the defile, and turn their stock on the heavy grass that grew along the base of the Sandias and Manzanos. All of the prospective settlers had families, except bachelor Joseph Antonio Baca. Before he could be confirmed as a grantee, the governor ordered him to "marry for the increase and concord of the settlement." Since Baca wanted his land, he quickly hunted up a bride and got married.

On February 12, 1763, the assistant alcalde of Albuquerque accompanied the people to their grant, where they went through the familiar ceremony of possession. Boundaries of the tract were delineated and house lots assigned to individuals. The new village, established near the mouth of the canyon, was formally named San Miguel de Laredo, but because of its location, most people called it San Miguel de Carnué, or simply Carnué.

Ethnically, the settlers were a mixed lot. In addition to the Spaniards, there were several *coyotes,* that is, mixed bloods, and a handful of genízaros, the Hispanicized Indians who formed a kind of floating population in many New Mexican towns. Carnué had no church, or any public official, so it was dependent for its religious and political needs upon the villa of Albuquerque, twelve miles away. The lack of any supervising agency left the residents to stray, when they chose, from the straight paths of lawful behavior. In 1763, for example, they were accused of illegally trading with Apaches who had come to the doorstep of the village to swap salt, corn, and deerskins for horses and cattle. Albuquerque's assistant alcalde, Baltasar Griego, who had known about the trade but kept quiet, was arrested and sent to Santa Fe, where he spent three days in the guardhouse. He was jailed mainly because he neglected to require the Carnué men to get the proper business license.

A more serious incident occurred in the spring of 1768. Two of Carnué's genízaros were taken into custody by provincial authorities on charges of cattle rustling. At their trial in April, they confessed to taking animals from the pueblo of Zia on the Jemez River, but declared they had been put up to it by their Spanish neighbors who were trafficking in stolen stock. The pair was sentenced to labor on public works at low pay until they had earned enough to make restitution for the cattle. Their Spanish accomplices got off scot-free. The little episode suggests that the Carnué citizenry ran more toward the off-scourings of the frontier rather than toward the upright and moral folk one usually associates with pioneering ventures.

The people of the Middle Valley were eager to see Carnué succeed. Situated as it was near the opening of the only pass through the eastern mountains, the struggling little village offered a first line of defense for the villa of Albuquerque. Some of the less belligerent Apache bands, as we have indicated, were willing to trade peacefully at Carnué, but others saw the village as a golden opportunity for indulging their appetite for robbery and murder. In 1770 a flurry of raids occurred, culminating during October in a major assault on the community. Several of the settlers fell and the disheartened survivors bundled up their families and fled back to Albuquerque.

Upon receiving the dismal news that Carnué had been abandoned, Governor Pedro Fermín de Mendinueta ordered the people to return or face loss of their grant. Thirteen of the braver souls, though poorly armed and insufficiently provisioned, gave it a try, but they lasted only two days before scurrying anew for the relative safety of Albuquerque. In a letter addressed to the governor, sent in early April of 1771, they attempted to explain their loss of heart. The place was swarming with Apaches, the letter said. Four of the settlers did not even have weapons, and few as they were, it was impossible "to oppose the great boldness which the barbarous enemy now displays." Hungry and broken in spirit they had given up.

Hard-fisted Governor Mendinueta viewed the matter in a different light. Perhaps recalling that the inhabitants of Carnué already possessed a blackened reputation owing to their shady dealings in the past, he now cited them for cowardice. In a stern decree (issued April 12, 1771), he charged that the settlers had grossly exaggerated the risk as a way to hide their own want of courage. To Don Francisco Treból Navarro, alcalde mayor of Albuquerque, he gave orders that unless Carnué was resettled at once, he was to nullify the grant and force its displaced citizens to hire out in the valley as laborers to prevent them from becoming vagrants.

Twelve days later, the Carnué grantees held a stormy meeting with Treból Navarro. It took place in the casas reales, or municipal buildings, on the Albuquerque plaza. Also in attendance was a new group of landless genízaros whom the alcalde, with a specific purpose in mind, had managed to round up. Knowing that they were good fighters, he attempted to persuade them to join the old settlers and reclaim Carnué where they would be given house lots and farms. If they all worked together, he assured the assembled throng, then the place could be retaken and held.

Hot debate produced near tumult there in the council chamber. The genízaros were unanimous in refusing to volunteer for so dangerous an enterprise. Nor did the alcalde receive even a particle of encouragement from the settlers. Nothing had changed, they wailed. Carnué was a death trap. They were not about to lose their lives at the hands of the Apaches as had already happened to some of their number the past October. As for the grant, they were prepared then and there to give up all rights to it. For them it had been an accursed gift. In the face of such determined opposition, Treból Navarro disbanded the meeting and acknowledged failure.

A few weeks later, he notified the former residents of Carnué to bring their wrecking tools and assemble at the casas reales in Albuquerque. On the appointed day, he led them out across the East Mesa to the silent walls of the town and set each man to demolishing his deserted house. By nightfall, the place was a pile of rubble. The New Mexican authorities wanted nothing left that might serve as a base of operations for roaming Apache war parties.

Governor Mendinueta was much put out by the whole affair and evidently hoped that he would hear no more of Carnué. The Albuquerqueans, on the other hand, still wished for some kind of outpost at the site to afford them a bit of security when they grazed their extensive flocks on El Llano, as they called the East Mesa. Therefore, they gave their full support to a new resettlement plan offered in 1774. The proposal to reestablish Carnué came from thirty-five families who had just been chased out of San Fernando and the Rio Puerco Basin. Adrift and out of work now in the Middle Valley, they selected Antonio Montaño, brother of Bernabé, to make their appeal to the governor. They also solicited the aid of Treból Navarro, who was enthusiastic about the idea but unhappy over the paltry material resources the petitioners could contribute to the project. As he apprised the governor, only five of the men owned muskets, the remainder having nothing more than spears, bows and arrows, clubs, and shields. That was precious little in the way of weaponry to stand off well-armed Apaches. To make matters worse, the thirty-five poverty-stricken families together possessed a mere twelve riding animals and eight ox teams. The numbers, as any experienced frontiersman could see, were far from enough to defend and sustain a new town.

That was Governor Mendinueta's conclusion, too. He had worries aplenty trying to protect his vast jurisdiction and the last thing he desired was the addition of another liability, which from past experience, he knew Carnué would turn out to be. Not unexpectedly, he denied the application for a new grant with the explanation that the settlers failed to demonstrate that they had sufficient arms and provisions to carry through. And that was that—for the moment, at any rate.

Carnué, in fact, was not resurrected until well into the nineteenth century. A group of Albuquerque citizens in 1818 applied for a grant in the canyon, and since the Apache threat had subsided, it was approved. They built a new San Miguel de Carnué just inside the mouth of the pass and went to farming the tiny patches of flatland strung along the creek. Eastward above the Tijeras, where the canyon forked, other settlers entered the following year and founded the village of San Antonio. Thus, by the end of the colonial period in 1821, three miles of the canyon floor were under cultivation.

All of this shifting about of people and expansion of settlement in and around Albuquerque was typical of the entire colonial period. Every bit of good land within the villa was preempted during the first decade or so following 1706 and, thereafter, as population grew, colonists either had to make do with smaller farms or move farther out. In a small inbred community like Albuquerque, petty quarrels proliferated, and much of the bickering involved disputes over property boundaries. Knowing full well his fellow countrymen's penchant for fussing about land rights, Albuquerque's first alcalde, Martín Hurtado, when issuing grants, gave specific instructions that owners should avoid raising controversies. Those who did not, he promised to fine 20 pesos, the sum to be applied to the building of the church and the town jail. But for all the effect his order had, the alcalde might as well have commanded the spring winds to cease blowing. Boundary squabbles, leading to bitter family feuds and endless litigation, irritated Albuquerque's early social life like recurring canker sores.

The chronic shortage of farmland was exacerbated by the hostile Indian problem—people afraid to appear in the fields and plow oxen lost to raiders—and by periodic droughts, which left insufficient irrigation water to go around. Crops failed completely due to drought at least three times between 1714 and 1734. Under those stressful conditions, it is scarcely surprising that, periodically, tempers flared and men picked fights with their neighbors. The colonial court records list cases that range from creating a public disturbance to homicide.

One incident, indicative of the times, took place during the summer of 1719. It involved respected members of the community—original founders of the villa—a fact that, when combined with the violent nature of the affair, promoted much raising of eyebrows and tongue wagging. Don Nicolás de

Chávez, scion of one of the oldest families in the Middle Valley, was at the center of the rumpus. Son of Fernando Durán y Chávez, former alcalde mayor of Bernalillo and developer of large properties at Atrisco, Don Nicolás had expanded his patrimony to include lands on the southern limits of Albuquerque and in the Isleta area. Prosperity and an aristocratic lineage—the Chávez were descended from a noble family of Spain—produced in him an attitude of haughtiness and a corresponding disdain for others' sensibilities. But in the summer of which we speak, he was still in his late twenties, so that some of what followed may actually be attributed to the hotheadedness characteristic of youth.

The man who raised Don Nicolás's ire, thereby becoming the second protagonist in the story, was seventy-year-old Pedro López. His farm, the southernmost within the nebulous boundaries of Albuquerque, lay near the Camino Real and adjacent to the brushy quagmires of Mejía. The citizens of the villa, as previously noted, were accustomed to turn their livestock loose to graze the lush grasses of the swamp, and evidently some of the animals were wont to stray from time to time into the unfenced fields of Pedro López. On the occasion in question, Don Nicolás had ridden down to check on his roaming cattle and, while about it, he had run into López.

Harsh words were exchanged. The older man ordered Chávez to remove his cows from the vicinity, claiming they had trespassed on his farm. Don Nicolás refused. He could see no damage that had been done, and suggested that if there were some, then Pedro López should take the matter to court. The argument grew in intensity. It finally became violent.

Each man claimed later that the other had seized a stick

and struck the first blow. Chávez belabored López and vice versa. In the midst of the altercation, the elder's son, Pedro Acenzio López, dashed up. An Indian servant had come running to his house crying that somebody was beating his father to death with a stick. Grabbing his sword he had leaped on a horse and rushed to the rescue.

On arrival, Pedro Acenzio recalled afterward, he politely greeted Don Nicolás with a *Buenas tardes* and removed his sombrero. Dismounting, he asked him why he was attacking his father, an old man ill and weighted down with years. Chávez responded insolently and brandished his stick, whereupon the son met him with a sword thrust. At that point, Don Nicolás dropped his makeshift weapon and took to his heels.

True enough that Pedro Acenzio had doffed his hat, Chávez reported, but then he launched an unprovoked attack inflicting a stab wound. He had fled into the dense underbrush of the bosque and there armed himself with a larger stick. Returning again to the open fields, he met Pedro Acenzio and they renewed their combat. Old Pedro López, his grandson, and several neighbors now came up and joined the melee. Don Nicolás sustained another cut from his opponent's sword, and his clothes were soon drenched with blood. López, the father, looked scarcely better for blood gushed from his mouth and nose as a result of his earlier drubbing. Someone might have been killed but for the timely intervention of Captain Alonso García, who chanced to be passing by along the Camino Real on his way from Isleta to Albuquerque. Seeing the tumult, he galloped up and put a stop to the whole affray. The captain took Chávez up behind him on his horse, together they went in search of the Don's mount, and then they rode into Albuquerque to get medical attention.

The matter was serious enough to warrant the governor sending a judicial investigator, Alonso Rael de Aguilar, down from Santa Fe to conduct a formal inquiry. He collected testimony from Pedro López at his farm, from Nicolás de Chávez, convalescing in his home, and from the other witnesses. But getting to Pedro Acenzio, he who had carved up Don Nicolás with a sword, took a little doing, for after the assault, the son had taken refuge in the Albuquerque church, claiming the Spanish right of sanctuary. This meant that as long as he stayed inside the church, no law officer could arrest him.

Rael de Aguilar knew, however, that if he obtained the consent of the local minister, he was allowed to enter and take a statement from the fugitive. But the right of sanctuary also allowed the fugitive to refuse to answer, if he chose, by repeating the phrase "church is my name" to all questions. "Going to the friary of Nuestro Padre San Francisco," Rael de Aguilar says, "I requested with all kindness and due courtesy of the Reverend Father Andrés de Zevallos that as a good servant of His Majesty he should grant me permission to go into the church, and he graciously assented."

As it turned out, Pedro Acenzio was willing to waive his right to answer "church is my name" (equivalent to the modern practice of taking the Fifth Amendment), and consequently the investigator was able to get a declaration from the last witness. When his work was completed, Rael de Aguilar submitted the entire record of the proceedings to the governor who, in addition to his political and military duties, served in effect as the chief justice of the province. The judgment he handed down seems relatively mild, given the amount of blood that had been spilled: both Pedro Acenzio López and Nicolás de Chávez were fined, the money going into the building fund for the Albuquerque church. To boot, Don Nicolás was instructed to keep a closer watch over his livestock hereafter. And so the case was closed.

Though but one small incident of mayhem in the history of the villa, it tells us something about the nature of those all too human Albuquerqueans of the eighteenth century—about their fierce Spanish pride, which showed when a personal insult was involved, and their quickness to anger and to take up arms against a neighbor. Naturally, not everyone went for a stick or a sword at the first sign of a disagreement; most, in accepted fashion, carried their problems to court. Even there, however, the records are sufficiently complete to suggest that during the long years of the Spanish regime the waters beneath the seemingly placid surface of Albuquerque's social life were fraught with discord.

The Chávez-López squabble pitted the stockman, who turned out his animals to graze at will, against the farmer, forced to be on guard constantly lest wandering cattle and horses devour his unfenced crops. It was a familiar problem, like the persistent haggles over land boundaries. With stockraising and agriculture as the twin mainstays of the villa's economy, some competition between the two occupations was no doubt inevitable. The rancher, as in any society of Spaniards, enjoyed greater standing in the community than did the farmer. His flashy dress and prancing horse set him apart. And the size of his herds and flocks proved an easily visible measure of his wealth, as is still the case among the Navajo, who accumulate livestock to enhance their reputations in the tribe.

Much of Albuquerque's colonial population consisted of subsistence farmers who raised enough for their family's needs, with maybe a tiny surplus in good years that could be traded at nearby pueblos or in Santa Fe, two days' journey to the north. The Albuquerque census for 1790, the most detailed one we have for the colonial era, lists fifty-seven farmers, and only four ranchers. Across the river, however, little Atrisco had twelve ranchers and but seven farmers. The emphasis on stockraising there can be attributed to the dearth of farmlands on the west side of the river and, conversely, to the abundance of pasture stretching league upon league toward the Puerco Basin. Given the high proportion of ranchers at Atrisco, it would not be amiss to suppose that the place was regarded as a "prestige suburb" of Albuquerque.

Although both cattle and sheep were raised in the Middle Valley and its environs, most people engaged in ranching strongly favored sheep. One reason was that cows were easily stampeded by hostile Indians and, if captured, they could be driven away swiftly. Sheep, being slower of foot, were somewhat less attractive to raiders. Also, the shepherds had the habit when attacked of scattering their flocks, a practice that seemed to cut down on losses.

Many sheep raisers turned their flocks over to herders on shares, the so-called *partido* system. The shepherd (called a *partidario*) entered into a contract with the owner, agreeing to pasture and care for the sheep year-round in exchange for a specified share of the increase. From the flock he got meat and milk to feed his family and plenty of wool to be spun into yarn for blankets and clothing. The drawback was that out of his share he had to make up for animals lost to Indians, wolves, or rattlesnakes. Many of the men who went with Bernabé Montaño to settle the Puerco country were partidarios who drove sheep belonging to ranchers in the Middle Valley. But the Navajos cut into the flocks so deeply that most of the partidarios went broke, one of the reasons they later abandoned their homes and came back to Albuquerque.

In the beginning, even the most prosperous owners had no more than a few hundred head of *ganado menor* (small stock), by which was meant flocks of sheep with a few goats mixed in. For instance, Josepha Baca, a well-to-do widow and mistress of an hacienda at Pajarito just below Albuquerque, in 1746 claimed ownership of 600 ganado menor, all let out on shares to residents of the Rio Abajo. At the same time, another rancher of the district, Luís García, brother of Captain Alonso García, listed 747 sheep and goats in his possession. As the years advanced the size of the flocks grew larger in spite of the toll taken by Indians. Aristocratic Manuel Durán de Armijo of Albuquerque in 1764 made provision in his will for over 1,200 head of sheep and goats; and that was in addition to 24 plow oxen and more than 100 cows and bulls. By the opening of the nineteenth century, sheep were plentiful and the standard size of each flock let to partidarios came to be 1,000 ewes and 10 breeding rams.

Very little hard money circulated among the colonial New Mexicans and, as a consequence, sheep, valued at one to two pesos depending upon the period, customarily served as a unit of exchange. There existed a great temptation on the part of ranchers to ship as much wool clip and as many sheep as possible for sale to the presidios and mining communities of northern New Spain. But in the early years after Albuquerque's founding, the royal governors clamped tight controls on export of both products, as well as on grain and cattle, fearing that New Mexicans would be left short. While well intentioned, the prohibition placed a severe strain on the provincial economy. In 1737 Albuquerqueans got up a petition asking for relief: they desperately needed to sell more than woven blankets and stockings and piñon nuts in the Chihuahua markets. The ban continued, nevertheless, and it brought them in 1744 to a small crisis.

During that year, Albuquerque suffered an infestation of moths, and the hungry insects were attacking large stores of raw wool that the citizens had accumulated. Unable to sell the fiber locally, because of a temporary glut on the market, they were on the point of losing their entire investment. Then a heaven-sent opportunity appeared. Francisco de Vargas, manager of a large mule train from Mexico City, arrived in Albuquerque by way of the Camino Real. He represented himself as an agent for a wealthy merchant of the capital and he announced that he was prepared to purchase all the wool he could get hold of. The rub, of course, was that the Albuquerqueans could not sell without violating the law.

In an urgent letter to the governor at Santa Fe, they related the details of their moth problem and begged permission to turn their surplus wool while they had the chance. Fortunately, the governor was a man of flexible nature, not completely bound by the iron chains of bureaucracy, so he suspended for the moment the usual restriction on exports. But he stated clearly that his action applied to the present emergency only. Not until later in the century did the controls finally come off, leaving the people of New Mexico free to dispose of their goods unhindered.

The Camino Real, the principal artery of travel and trade, connecting New Mexico with the southern provinces, proved one of Albuquerque's leading economic assets, even in those first years when the volume of exports was severely limited. Caravans and pack trains, like the one from Mexico City headed by Francisco de Vargas, as a matter of course, passed through the villa on their way to Santa Fe and points beyond. The road was of equal significance to intraprovincial traffic, tying together, as it did, the Rio Abajo and the Rio Arriba. Sooner or later, everyone in New Mexico who had business that took him away from home passed through Albuquerque.

By an order dated October 12, 1732, the New Mexican governor directed alcaldes throughout the land to inform their citizens that the annual trade convoy would leave for Mexico on the following November 1. Those with goods to sell (legal goods, that is) should rendezvous at Albuquerque, where they would be provided a military escort for the dangerous trip down the Camino Real. He also reminded the alcaldes that everyone who planned to go was obliged to obtain a travel permit, another one of the many petty restrictions imposed upon Spanish subjects.

Departure of the merchant convoys, loaded with local products, was an annual event. In those years when the assembly point was Albuquerque, the villa's plaza for a few brief days in the fall became a scene of bustling activity. Most of what went on in the way of preparation must, unhappily, be left to our imagination, for no traveler of that colorful era, so far as we know, recorded his impressions in a diary or letters. As the area downriver from Albuquerque sprouted new settlements, the rendezvous shifted southward. For a time in the latter eighteenth century, the favored site was La Joya, a village on the east bank of the Rio Grande below Belen. Albuquerque, besides sending many of its people with the caravans as traders, also contributed, when requested by the governor, some of its militia to reinforce the regular soldiers who served as a mobile guard.

From all reports, finished textiles constituted the chief commodity produced in Albuquerque and sold in the *tierra afuera,* the "outside country"—at least until export of sheep and wool were freed from mercantile restraints late in the colonial period. Father Miguel de Menchero, writing in 1744, mentions that the principal occupations of the one hundred families who then comprised the combined populations of Albuquerque and Atrisco were farming and "weaving hose and blankets." That he failed to include stockraising is evidently an oversight on his part, for it was a relative abundance of sheep that made possible the thriving weaving industry. By 1790, as the census records show, Albuquerque supported forty-seven weavers, twenty-five carders, and fifteen spinners. Other villages and towns in the Middle Valley listed additional persons dedicated to these trades, so it is apparent that textile production was the chief cottage industry of the region. Second in importance, though far down the line, was shoemaking, with thirteen cobblers counted in Albuquerque. Their products, the New Mexican moccasins or teguas, were sold mainly within the province, but some were also exported to Chihuahua and Sonora.

From the beginnings of Albuquerque down to the end of

Spanish rule in 1821, the villa experienced slow but steady population growth. Over the years a number of censuses were compiled by military officers, alcaldes, and missionaries, but many of them are unreliable either because of the haphazard manner in which they were made, or because the taker failed to state whether his figures applied to the villa alone, or included adjacent villages under its jurisdiction.

Each new governor at the start of his administration was required by law to conduct a *visita,* or general inspection, of every town and village in New Mexico. In the course of his tour, he heard complaints from citizens, reviewed the militia, and took a census. The population data obtained during these formal visitas was generally far more accurate than that from other sources. But unfortunately, only a few of the governors' censuses survive.

One that we do have, taken by Governor Fernando de la Concha in 1789, is worth quoting in full as it provides interesting disclosures about the composition and character of Albuquerque's colonial population. On October 3 the governor summoned the villa's people to assemble and be counted, and at the same time he had the local militia march in review. The military parade must have been something less than inspiring since Concha wrote tersely in his log: "Out of the entire population, I considered only 220 fit for war, and of these only a very small number were properly mounted and armed. All the rest appeared in a most deplorable condition."

The census figures collected by the governor represent the number of inhabitants in Albuquerque and fourteen dependent plazas in the valley above and below the villa. They are as follows:

| Men over the age of 60 | 15 |
| Married men | 226 |
| Widowers | 16 |
| Bachelors | 126 |
| Boys 14 years and under | 293 |
| | |
| Women over the age of 60 | 17 |
| Married women | 233 |
| Widows | 60 |
| Unmarried women | 147 |
| Girls 12 years and under | 214 |
| *Total* | 1347 |

The discrepancy between the number of married men and women, which should have been the same, is not explained by the records.

From this data, several interesting facts emerge. One is that more than one-third of the population are children. Boys of 15 and older are counted as bachelors until they marry, usually in their early 20s, while girls 13 and older are listed as unmarried women, which explains the large figures in those categories. People over the age of 60, a total of 32, compose less than 5 percent of the population. Thus, the average lifespan of these early Albuquerqueans fell somewhere between 30 and 40 years, as was true in much of the western world at the time. How that somber fact affected the thought and outlook of the villa's residents we can scarcely calculate.

One other point bears noting. As Governor Concha's census demonstrates, widows outnumbered widowers nearly four to one. The higher mortality rate among men was probably owing, at least partially, to deaths at the hands of Indians while tending stock, doing militia duty on campaigns, and serving as escorts for the trade caravans. The possibility also exists that males suffered more fatalities from epidemic disease, which periodically ravaged the Rio Grande Valley.

Now that epidemics of infectious disease have largely been brought under control, it is difficult to recall the catastrophic effects they once had on colonial society. Church burial records, which show sudden spurts in the number of deaths during a major epidemic, bear the grim testimony. Measles depleted the ranks of children on several occasions. The common cold and acute respiratory diseases—pleurisy and pneumonia—were widespread. Impure water drawn from irrigation ditches was the source of dysentery and typhoid. Body lice, prevalent among the New Mexico population until well into the nineteenth century, carried typhus fever. But of the leading ailments, none was more feared or more deadly than smallpox, *el peste* as the Spanish folk knew it.

From the days of earliest settlement, smallpox seems to have been endemic among settlers on the Upper Rio Grande. The annual spring outbreak was usually a mild one, but about every ten years or so the disease would gather strength and burst forth in a particularly virulent form, causing great loss of life. In 1780, when a terrible pandemic of smallpox reached across the Southwest, thousands of people, many of them Indians, succumbed to the pestilence. In Albuquerque, thirty-one persons died, and during another flare-up the following year fifteen more, including four children, perished.

Because the scourge was so common and highly contagious, New Mexicans expected inevitably to come down with the disease. Statistics compiled in 1805 by Albuquerque's alcalde mayor, Manuel de Arteaga, convey an accurate picture of the magnitude of the problem. The larger Albuquerque district then had a total population, Arteaga reported to the governor, of 6,930. Of these, 2,202 were children under twelve years of age, of whom only 929 had not had smallpox. Among the remaining 4,728 people, only one had not been afflicted.

These gruesome figures represent the survivors. Since the fatality rate in a smallpox epidemic could range anywhere from 10 to 50 percent of those infected, we have to assume that in the several decades before 1805, hundreds of Albuquerqueans had fallen victim to the disease. If we were able to travel in a time machine back to that year, surely one of the first things catching our attention would be the faces of the people, all bearing the disfiguring scars of smallpox. Some folk, especially comely young women, tried to hide the pitted skin on their cheeks by liberal application of a red mineral paint or white flour as a cosmetic. But to our modern taste, that artifice would probably have appeared more grotesque than the honest scars of disease.

Even as Alcalde Arteaga was gathering his statistics, however, relief was on the way. Back in 1798 Englishman Edward Jenner had discovered an effective vaccine, made from cowpox virus, which rendered humans immune from smallpox. Recognizing the importance of this breakthrough, the Spanish king in late 1803 equipped an "expedition against smallpox" to sail around the world and distribute the precious vaccine to his colonial subjects and to all others who desired it. The vaccine was carried in the arms of six orphans and each eight days it was passed in relay to six others, so that the fluid remained fresh and available. In this way, the vaccine was disseminated via groups of children until it was carried throughout the Spanish empire.

By the summer of 1804, it had reached Chihuahua City, where Dr. Cristóbal Larrañaga, military surgeon from Santa Fe, was waiting to claim his share of vaccine for the people on the Upper Rio Grande. By the following winter, he was moving slowly northward from El Paso vaccinating as he went. All those he treated were children, for they were about the only ones who had not already had the disease. Those living through a bout of smallpox gained lifelong immunity, and hence did not need the vaccine.

At Albuquerque, Dr. Larrañaga vaccinated 37 children. He would have done more, but dysentery, measles, and whooping cough were all raging at the time and he dared not administer the vaccine to sick youngsters since it created a mild infection of its own. At intervals over the next ten years, however, he returned to the villa to continue the immunization program. Records dating from 1810, for example, indicate that in that year he vaccinated in the villa proper and six neighboring hamlets 124 children, ages 1 to 6 years.

In Spain and the rest of Europe, introduction of Jenner's vaccine brought a rapid fall in the death rate and led to an accelerated growth in population. A similar phenomenon can be noted for New Mexico generally and for the Albuquerque area in particular. During the first half of the nineteenth century, the population of the province more than doubled. While some of the increment can be attributed to immigration, the greater part may well be credited to an ongoing program of vaccination against the dreaded killer smallpox.

In the face of sickness and the constant threat of Indian raid, Albuquerque's people found solace in religion, which has always been the touchstone of Hispanic life. For the first few years after the villa was founded, and while the first church was slowly going up, they were ministered to by the priest at Bernalillo. As remarked, the church was constructed largely of adobes donated by local citizens or given by them as fines for various infractions of the law. By 1718 or so, the building seems to have been far enough along that services could be held, and the residence of the priest, the *convento,* was probably complete, or nearly so. In the early 1750s, Father Manuel José Rojo added a walled cemetery in front, with a large wooden cross standing on an adobe platform at the center. This same sort of arrangement, in which worshippers must walk through the cemetery to enter the main door of the church, can be seen today at some of the Pueblo Indian missions.

Fray Francisco Atanasio Domínguez inspected the Albuquerque church in 1776 and left us a full account of its appearance, furnishings, and operation. The structure faced east toward the Sandia Mountains and fronted upon a large rectangular plaza. There were no bell towers but at the top of the facade a small adobe arch had been erected to hold two bells, both of them cracked. Hewn beams and carved corbels supported the roof. Upon entering, one passed under the choir loft, a kind of balcony at the east end of the nave, facing the sanctuary. The space above the high altar was decorated with a painted screen containing pictures of the saints. Four side altars, two on the left and two on the right, a crudely put together confessional, a pulpit, and a baptismal font near the door completed the furnishings. Pews were absent: the congregation stood or knelt on the hard packed-dirt floor, women on the right side of the invisible aisle, men on the left.

The quick eye of Father Domínguez took note, during his brief visit, of the "lethargy and laziness" displayed by some Albuquerque parishioners toward their religious duties. His observation is reminiscent of Governor Marín del Valle's earlier complaint that Albuquerqueans were extremely care-less in the guarding of their livestock. These two statements suggest that apathy and a negligent attitude may have char-acterized life in the villa. That would help explain the aston-ishing fact that in the winter of 1792–1793 the people of Albuquerque allowed their church to collapse!

In a proclamation issued on February 18, 1793, Governor Fernando de la Concha referred to the occurrence as a public disgrace. He also spoke of the urgent necessity of getting the church back up and lamented the paltry resources of the parish. To accomplish the task at hand, he ordered everyone in the Middle Valley to pitch in, either with labor or contri-butions. So the message would get around, he directed that copies of his proclamation be posted in the convento of Albuquerque, at Isleta Pueblo, Belen, and Tomé.

Exactly what brought about the fall of the church is not revealed. Apparently earlier in 1792, it had shown signs of distress, for the villa's alcalde mayor had solicited help from local residents in making repairs. Adobe structures need constant maintenance—replastering the walls, mending of the packed-earth roof, attending to drainage around the founda-tions. The villa's citizenry probably let these things slide so far that their minor repairs failed to forestall the disaster and provoked the governor's charge of "a public disgrace."

The wreck must have been complete because plans were formulated at once to begin construction of an entirely new building, *"un nuevo edificio"* in Concha's words. Inexplicably, the builders failed to clear the rubble and restore the church to its original site. Instead they moved around to the north side of the plaza and commenced work on a structure that faced south. The project, likely extending over a period of years, produced a church quite unlike the original one viewed by Father Domínguez in 1776. The new building lacked the walled cemetery in front, but it was conspicuously graced with twin bell towers at each corner. It also had an interior in the form of a cross, with a shallow apse behind the sanctuary and transepts on either side. The former church, by contrast, had possessed a simple rectangular plan.

The San Felipe de Neri Church, begun in 1793, is the one that stands today in Albuquerque's Old Town Plaza. After almost two centuries of remodelings and additions, it bears scant resemblance to the original, yet under a false ceiling and beneath layers of paint and cement plaster, there remains much of the early fabric put in place by the villa's colonial residents.

Until almost the very close of the Spanish period, Albuquerque's religious ministry was in the hands of members of the Franciscan Order. The Franciscans, of course, were missionaries, having come initially with Juan de Oñate to convert the Pueblo Indians. Since they were the only priests in the province, they also took care of the spiritual needs of the colonists. Practically all their expenses were paid by the royal treasury, including the annual stipend for each missionary of 330 pesos. Understandably, this proved a serious financial strain on the government, which was nevertheless willing to shoulder the burden as it offered the best means for "civilizing" the Indians and incorporating them into the Spanish social and political system.

The intent always was that as soon as the Indian people had been fully converted, the missionaries were to be withdrawn and their place taken by ordinary, or secular, priests under authority of a bishop. With that change, the Indian parishioners were then expected to pay the salary and living expenses of their minister, as was the custom in any community of Spanish Catholics.

In New Mexico, as well as in other provinces on the northern frontier, the missionaries proved to be a stumbling block in carrying through this plan. Having become well entrenched, they were loath to give up their churches and congregations to the Johnny-come-lately secular priests. Therefore, they simply reported year after year that the Indians were not completely converted and that missionary work must go on. That meant also, as they were well aware, that their nice government stipends would continue.

The Franciscans found it much more difficult to justify their prolonged ministry in the Spanish towns. In its first years when New Mexico was a poor and struggling province, the royal treasury was willing to underwrite expenses for new churches and their priests as one means to help the colonists. But the government's charity had limits. It wanted the subsidized missionaries out as soon as possible, and secular priests in, who would be supported by the local parish.

To that end, an order was promulgated in the year 1767 calling for the replacement of the Franciscan friars in New Mexico's four villas of Santa Fe, Santa Cruz de la Cañada, Albuquerque, and El Paso with secular priests to be sent by the Bishop of Durango. The Diocese of Durango, of which New Mexico was a part, covered a vast area of the northern frontier. Its bishop, residing in the city of Durango, about eight hundred miles south of Santa Fe, generally showed little interest in his subjects in the remote Upper Rio Grande Valley, although at least two holders of that office did make a tour of New Mexico during their terms. The first was Bishop Benito Crespo y Monroy, who passed through Albuquerque on his way to Santa Fe in 1730. The second, Bishop Pedro Tamarón y Romeral, stopped at the villa on May 21, 1760, long enough to hold ecclesiastical ceremonies and to record in his journal one of the problems faced by the resident priest.

"Because some of his parishioners are on the other side of the river," wrote the bishop, "this parish priest of Albuquerque, called Fray Manuel Rojo, is obliged to cross it when summoned. This kept him under apprehension, and above all he emphasized to me that when the river froze, it was necessary to cross on the ice. He elaborated this point by saying that when the ice thundered, he thought he was on the way to the bottom, because when one crosses it, it creaks as if it were about to break."

The order of 1767 obliging the Bishop of Durango to send priests to New Mexico's villas was only partially implemented because of the shortage of clergy. Secular priests did take over in Santa Fe and El Paso, but Franciscans were left, at least for a time, to administer the churches of Albuquerque and Santa

Cruz de la Cañada. At both places, however, the government suspended the fathers' stipend, forcing them to depend for their livelihoods upon money exacted from the congregations. The main revenues came from fees (generally referred to as "offerings"), which the priests collected for baptisms, marriages, funerals, and other spiritual activities. They also charged extra for the privilege of burial inside the church. The going rates, given by Father Domínguez for Albuquerque, were: 4 pesos for burial at the back of the church, 8 pesos in the center; and 16 pesos up front near the sanctuary steps. Such marketing of services, an old practice in the Spanish Church, was later to shock the newly arrived Anglo-Americans.

Finally, in 1802, Bishop Francisco Olivares appointed one of his priests, Juan José de Sida, to go to Albuquerque and replace the Franciscan there, Fray Ambrosio Guerra. For fifteen years, Guerra had ministered to Albuquerqueans, and it must have been with pangs of regret that he departed the villa for a new post. If so, his grief was of short duration, for less than two years later Father Sida was recalled to Durango and Guerra was reassigned to Albuquerque.

He was there in 1806 when the villa passed its first century mark (no evidence exists that Albuquerque took note of the occasion), and he was still there the following year when a young army lieutenant from the United States, Zebulon Montgomery Pike, passing down the Camino Real stopped by the San Felipe convento to pay him a social call. For a hundred years, Albuquerque had been a small backwater villa in the Spanish empire, but the day of Hispanic rule was fast approaching an end. Neither Father Ambrosio Guerra nor Lieutenant Pike, as they sat amiably conversing in the priest's quarters, had any inkling of that fact, for as yet no hint was in the air of the profound transformations that would soon shake Albuquerque and all New Mexico. For the moment it was enough that a hospitable Spanish priest and an eager American officer should enjoy each other's company and sip wine there in the largest town of the Rio Grande's Middle Valley.

# 4

# The Winds of Change

FROM THE DAYS of Ferdinand and Isabella, Spain and its overseas colonies lay under the tight control of the crown. The succession of kings in the seventeenth and eighteenth centuries reigned as absolute monarchs, exercising the last word in political, judicial, economic, military, and even church matters. Through a vast network of officials, the sovereign kept tabs on his subjects everywhere in the huge empire. And an enormous body of royal laws regulated the smallest details of human activity.

One portion of those laws, imposing a strict prohibition on foreign trade, had a serious impact upon New Mexico in the late colonial period. As the province grew in population and its economy expanded, it desperately needed new markets for its raw products and new and cheaper sources for imported manufactured goods. But under the existing system, the New Mexicans were permitted to do business only within New Spain, which meant all their trade had to be funneled down the Camino Real to the city of Chihuahua, five hundred miles south of Albuquerque. As early as 1778, Father Juan Augustín de Morfí called attention to the inequities that resulted.

"The people of New Mexico," he pointed out, "are truly puppets of the Chihuahua merchants, from whom they get credit to run their own businesses and to whom they must repay with raw products of the country. The Chihuahuans, knowing perfectly well the ins and outs of this commerce, overcharge for the goods they sell and knock down prices on what they buy. As a consequence, there is scarcely any margin with which the New Mexicans can pay freight and still support themselves, even at a poverty level. Since they have no alternative, they are forced to accept the rules laid down in Chihuahua."

The best way for New Mexico to break this onerous monopoly would have been to open trade with French, British, and later, American merchants in the Mississippi Valley. But that practical course was effectively blocked by stern royal laws, which kept the gates at the borders of the empire firmly locked. Several small parties of Frenchmen did sneak into New Mexico to barter their wares in the years after 1740, but their few illegal intrusions did little to satisfy the local hunger for foreign goods.

Then in 1803 France sold the vast Louisiana Territory to the United States. That brought the new American nation to the very edge of northern New Mexico and raised the prospect of a foreign market being developed close at hand. Spain, however, gave no sign of dropping her long-standing trade barriers. Indeed, nervous over America's headlong

expansion, she tightened her restrictive policies and redou-
bled her watchfulness.

Lieutenant Zebulon Pike was the first American to fall
afoul of the Spanish law against trespassers. Handsome and
dashing, the twenty-six-year-old officer in 1806 was placed in
command of a small party to explore the headwaters of the
Arkansas and Red rivers. Those streams, it was thought then,
formed the boundary between the Louisiana Purchase and
New Spain. Late in the year, Pike crossed the plains to the foot
of the Colorado Rockies where he and his men made camp
and shivered through a miserable winter. With the spring
thaw, they crossed the mountains and Pike ordered construction of a small stockade on the Conejos River, an affluent of
the Rio Grande. He professed to believe that he was on the
upper reaches of the Red River and, hence, inside territory of
the United States. But that notion was quickly dispelled by a
force of one hundred Spaniards, who marched up from Santa
Fe and took the American intruders into custody.

There is some reason to think that Lieutenant Pike actually invited capture as the best means for gaining admittance
to New Mexico and seeing what lay behind the Spanish veil.
If that was the case, then the ploy worked, for during his
enforced tour of the Upper Rio Grande Valley, he got an eyeful.

The Spaniards were a model of courtesy. At Santa Fe,
Governor Joaquin Real Alencaster questioned Pike at length
concerning his motives and intentions and dined him in the old
mud palace facing the plaza. It was not like a captivity at all,
for the Americans were allowed to keep their personal possessions, including sidearms, and to explore the streets of the capital. Later the governor informed Pike that he was sending them

with an escort to Chihuahua City for further interrogation by the commander general. Alencaster made clear, however, that the Americans were going as guests of the Spanish government, not as prisoners of war. To show his friendly intent, he hitched up his state coach with six mules, invited Lieutenant Pike inside, and accompanied him several miles on the road leading south from Santa Fe.

At the end of the first week of March 1807, Pike, his men, and the military escort reached Albuquerque. Throughout the Middle Valley people were at work opening and cleaning the irrigation ditches in preparation for spring planting. "We saw," Pike recalled afterward, "men, women and children of all ages at the joyful labor which was to crown with rich abundance their future harvests and ensure them plenty for the ensuing year. Those scenes brought to my recollection the bright descriptions . . . of the opening of the canals of Egypt. The cultivation of the fields was now commencing and everything appeared to give life and gaiety to the surrounding scenery." His words provide us the first reference to colonial Albuquerque by an American visitor.

Upon reaching the center of the villa, the officer and his companions were hospitably entertained by Father Ambrosio Guerra. Leading his guests into his own quarters, the priest introduced the members of the household, who, to the astonishment of the Americans, turned out to be beautiful young damsels. "Our host," wrote Pike, "ordered his adopted children of the female sex to appear, when they came in by turns, Indians, of various nations, Spanish, French, and finally, two young girls who from their complexion I conceived to be English." Noting that the two fair maidens had caught the officer's eye, Father Guerra directed them to give him a hug, as a mark of friendship, which they did most willingly. Then they sat with him on the sofa. To the flustered lieutenant, the priest explained that the girls had been seized somewhere in the east and traded from tribe to tribe. He had purchased them as infants and now they could recollect neither their names nor original language.

The party shortly sat down to dinner at a table bountifully supplied with a variety of dishes and an assortment of wines. Pike, somewhat breathless, declared eloquently: "We were waited on by a half dozen of those beautiful girls, who like Hebe at the feast of the gods, converted our wine to nectar, and with their ambrosial breath shed incense on our cups." For a young man fresh from the wilderness, the Roman-style banquet in the humble precincts of Albuquerque was as stimulating as it was unexpected.

With many expressions of thanks, Zebulon Pike took his leave of Father Guerra and continued his enforced march to Chihuahua, arriving there on April 2. Again he was subjected to prolonged interviews by the military authorities. But a few weeks later, he learned that his company was to be taken north and deposited in American territory at Natchitoches, Louisiana. Much to Pike's displeasure, Spanish officials decided to keep the bulk of his personal papers, including the maps and journals compiled during the preceding months of exploration.

Once again in the United States, Lieutenant Pike discovered that his fellow countrymen were keenly interested in what he had seen along the southern border of the Louisiana Purchase. From memory he assembled a report of his experiences and had it published in 1810. His work gave Americans their first inside view of Hispanic life and customs on the Rio Grande and demonstrated the bright trade prospects offered by New Mexico. The cost of manufactured goods throughout the province was exorbitant, Pike reported. Fine-quality textiles sold for twenty-five dollars per yard, and other imported articles were commensurately high. The message, for canny Yankee traders, was plain. The New Mexico market offered an untapped bonanza, but only if Spain's wall of restrictions on commerce and travel could be pierced. Pike's expedition had raised a tantalizing possibility, but more than a decade was to elapse before anyone in either the United States or New Mexico was to benefit from it.

When Lieutenant Zebulon Montgomery Pike visited Albuquerque and partook of Father Guerra's generous hospitality, he had no way of knowing that he represented the vanguard of an American wave that in the course of the century would storm the fortress of Hispanic culture on the Rio Grande. His appearance in the villa was a portent of change, but not all of the change the town was to experience, especially in those early years of the nineteenth century, derived from contact with the United States. The Spanish empire itself was in turmoil, the rigid system of an absolute monarchy under attack from within. Political upheaval in the mother country and in colonial New Spain sent ripples all the way to the northern frontier, touching the lives of Albuquerqueans and the residents of other communities in New Mexico.

The new era in Spain was ushered in by the Napoleonic Wars, which witnessed an invasion by French forces in the spring of 1808 and the capture of King Ferdinand VII. At the southern port city of Cádiz, which escaped occupation by the French, a regency was installed to rule until such time as Ferdinand could be returned to power. In 1810 that body issued a call for the meeting of a *cortes,* or congress, to be attended by representatives from each province in the empire. The liberal nature of the regency was underscored by one of its decrees, which declared that, henceforward, all citizens at home and abroad should consider themselves elevated to the status of free men. That revolutionary notion, growing out of liberal ideas emanating from France and the United States, was indeed a novel one for Spanish subjects, who for three centuries had been enchained by the absolute power of the monarchy.

In New Mexico, Don Pedro Bautista Pino, a distinguished resident of Santa Fe, was selected to travel to Spain and represent his province in the cortes. He arrived at Cádiz in time to assist in the promulgation, on March 18, 1812, of a new constitution for the empire. The document imposed strict curbs on the power of the king, whenever he should return to the throne, creating in effect a limited or constitutional monarchy. The cortes also issued a law directing all towns within the Spanish realm to elect municipal councils, called *ayuntamientos,* which could provide true representative government at the local level. It was this particular measure that had the most noticeable impact on Albuquerque.

By 1814, the villa had conducted an election, the first free balloting in its history, and installed an ayuntamiento. The council was composed of the required officials: magistrates, councilors, and a secretary. The neighboring communities of Bernalillo and Belen were also entitled to ayuntamientos, and their elections were carried out at about the same time as the one in Albuquerque.

Unhappily, this experiment in municipal democracy was short-lived. Napoleon suffered defeat and Ferdinand VII regained the Spanish throne. Looking askance at the liberal policies that had flowered in his absence, he promptly did away with the cortes and abolished the laws limiting his authority. Specifically, he ordered that the ayuntamientos be extinguished and that the former officials who had preceded them be returned to office. For Albuquerque, when it received the king's decree in 1815, this meant dissolving the elective council and reinstating the alcalde mayor, the appointive officer who had directed all the villa's affairs since its founding in 1706.

Ferdinand was badly out of touch, both with the times and his New World subjects. Spanish Americans, having tasted the sweet fruit of liberty, were in no mood to return to the autocratic rule of a pompous king. Abolition of the cortes and repeal of its enlightened laws helped spark independence movements throughout North and South America. After an interval of revolutionary wars in which his royal troops generally got the worst of it, Ferdinand made a belated attempt to save his empire by restoring, in 1820, the cortes and the constitution. His action was a classic case of too little, too late. Mainland America was lost to Spain, leaving her only Cuba and Puerto Rico in the Caribbean.

The Viceroyalty of New Spain broke with the empire in September of 1821, taking the name Mexico. Until a new form of government could be worked out, it was proclaimed that the Spanish constitution formulated by the cortes in 1812 should remain the law of the land. Ahead of Mexico lay years of political turbulence and instability, conditions that would affect the destiny of New Mexico far out on the northern rim of the new nation.

For Albuquerqueans, this drawn-out series of revolutionary events touched their lives only marginally. Workaday tasks associated with the changing of the seasons, which put bread and meat on the table, were of far greater concern than the marches and countermarches of distant armies and the heated speeches of remote politicians. No document has come to light confirming that the residents of the villa celebrated the consummation of independence with the ringing of church bells, firing of cannons, and the delivery of patriotic speeches as was done by their countrymen up in Santa Fe. But such may have been the case. They did, however, make one gesture of record: Albuquerque's plaza was formally named the Plaza de la Constitución. The town also got back its elective ayuntamiento, as did Bernalillo and Belen. Two other communities of the Middle Valley, Pajarito and Alameda, picked up municipal councils as well.

In September 1822, the Albuquerque ayuntamiento formulated a detailed census, probably the first taken following independence. From it, we are given one of our best glimpses of the early-day character of the villa's population. The ayuntamiento's secretary, Antonio Ruíz, who is author of the census, defined the area covered by the tabulations: "This jurisdiction [of Albuquerque] extends three leagues from north to south and thirteen leagues from east to west. It should be understood that [the area] in the latter direction is unpopulated, serving only for firewood collecting and pasturage." And he added, "The inhabitants are engaged in agriculture and the tending of their livestock. There is no industry whatsoever."

The population given for the Albuquerque jurisdiction is 2,302, of which 1,415 are unmarried males and females (this includes children), 796 are married persons, and 91 are widows and widowers. Of the total, more than half (1,361) are under the age of twenty-five. A separate listing of occupations shows: 297 farmers, 15 merchants, 13 craftsmen, 121 day laborers, 3 teachers, and 1 priest. An appended property valuation discloses 416 houses worth 5,006 pesos, and farmland (acreage not mentioned) valued at 7,181 pesos. If nothing else, such data illustrates that the area remained essentially rural in character, farmers and farm laborers far outnumbering the few members of the business, artisan, and professional class.

The quarter century (1821–1846) that New Mexico remained under the Republic of Mexico proved to be a period of innovation and revolutionary change. A faltering national government in Mexico City alternated between ill-advised intervention in New Mexico's internal affairs and gross neglect of her economic and defense problems. Beyond question, the province was more on its own during these years than it had ever been under the old Spanish regime.

One thing Albuquerqueans quickly noticed was that they were going to have to pay more heed to their own military security. A bankrupt national treasury and a Mexican army in disarray were able to provide even less aid in dealing with hostile Indians than that once supplied by Spain. Soon after independence, for example, moneys in the *fondo de aliados* dried up. This "alliance fund," long furnished by the royal government, had been used to purchase gifts for annual distribution to friendly tribes, such as the Comanches, Jicarilla Apaches, and the Utes. It served as the chief instrument in maintaining peace with those Indians, leaving the New Mexicans free to deal with the still unpacified southern Apaches and Navajos.

When the funds and gifts were cut off in 1821, the old alliances, especially the important one with the Comanches, were placed in jeopardy. Albuquerque and its sister communities on the Rio Grande wanted no return to those bitter days of warfare that had existed before Governor Anza struck a peace with the Comanche in 1786. But for a time, it appeared things might go just that way. In August of 1821, a band of Comanches showed up in Santa Fe seeking their accustomed allotment of gifts, but now they were turned away empty handed. Heading back for the plains, they vented their anger upon the village of San Miguel, where they killed livestock, sacked several homes, and raped two women. Governor Facundo Melgares, aware that this outrage might be a harbinger of things to come, circulated an appeal throughout New Mexico, soliciting donations from private citizens to replenish the alliance fund. His actions, which brought in some revenues, evidently forestalled any major breakdown of the Comanche peace, although stray members of the tribe made small raids on the Upper Rio Grande Valley during the decade of the 1820s.

The real threat to Albuquerque's security, however, came not from the Comanche, but from the Navajo, who were flexing new muscle beyond the Rio Puerco. After raiding Spanish flocks on the Rio Grande for two or more generations, the tribesmen had developed a pastoral economy based on the grazing of thousands of head of sheep. This placed them in direct competition for pasturage with stockmen from the Middle Valley, who kept edging westward looking for new ranges. As early as 1804 Spaniards out of the Albuquerque-Atrisco area had built the fortified settlement of Cebolleta on the eastern flank of Mount Taylor, in the very heart of Navajo country. Although more than once nearly overwhelmed by hostile Indians, the little town managed to hold its ground and survive.

By 1818 warfare between the New Mexicans and the Navajo was unremitting, and brutal in its intensity. Each side launched attacks on the other, slaying, stealing livestock, and taking captives. The battle-hardened men of Cebolleta soon came to specialize in the seizing of Navajo prisoners who could be sold as servants for 500 pesos apiece to wealthy landowners in Albuquerque. The Navajos, for their part, grabbed youngsters from the settlements, adopted them, and put them to herding sheep. This two-way traffic in human lives kept the flames of resentment burning at white heat.

In the early years of the nineteenth century, Albuquerque had begun to beef up her local militia. The ten-man contingent of Spanish soldiers that protected the town in its infancy and youth was long since gone, so that the ranks of volunteer troops, recruited in the immediate district, shouldered the full burden of defense. In 1815, fifty-year-old Captain Bartolomé Baca, a seasoned campaigner and soon-to-be governor of New Mexico, was listed as commander of Albuquerque's Cavalry Company of Volunteer Militia.

Four years later, a complete muster list was compiled of the villa's citizen forces, and it showed more than 360 officers and men under arms. Within the provincial-wide militia organization, Albuquerque's home guard was designated as the Second Squadron. It was comprised of three companies of cavalry totaling 150 men, plus a large infantry company with 212 members. Persons of wealth and influence, of course, gravitated to the cavalry, whose officer corps was dominated by the prominent Armijo family. The ranks of the infantry, under the command of Captain José Mariano de la Peña, were filled, in the main, by poor folk from the farming class.

As the tempo of strife with the Navajo increased in the years following independence, the role of the large Albuquerque militia assumed ever greater importance. It responded, for instance, to a general call-up issued in the summer of 1823 by then Governor José Antonio Vizcarra. Assembling an army of 1,500 men, the governor conducted a wide sweep through western New Mexico, killing 32 Navajos and taking 30 prisoners. Similar campaigns, undertaken periodically throughout the Mexican period, did little or nothing to check that tribe's harassment of the New Mexico frontier. Indeed, the Navajo remained a perennial menace to settlers in the Middle Valley until their final defeat by American soldiers in the mid-1860s.

The year 1821 proved a watershed, not only because it marked the formal break with Spain, but also because it signaled the opening of the overland trade with the United States. When William Becknell of Missouri reached Santa Fe in late summer at the head of a mule train loaded with merchandise, he found that Mexico, reversing the old restrictive policies of the colonial government, had flung open the door to foreign commerce. Disposing of his wares at a fat profit, he hastened home to restock and to spread the word that New Mexico was now welcoming Yankee merchants.

A minor rush followed as Americans pointed their caravans of white-topped freight wagons up the nine-hundred-mile-long trail to Santa Fe. Within two years, however, New Mexico was fairly glutted with American goods and the Missouri traders began looking southward toward Chihuahua and Durango in hopes of finding new markets. For many of them Santa Fe soon became not the end of the trail, but a waystation at the junction with the old Camino Real, which led on to Mexico's rich mining frontier. Albuquerque, handily situated astride the road south, found itself in a good position to benefit from the increased flow of traffic up and down the Rio Grande Valley.

Among pillars of the community who moved quickly to share in the booming commerce were Mariano Chávez and his brother, Antonio José. They were sons of Francisco Javier Chávez, a native of Belen and an influential voice in provincial politics. By this period, the 1820s, the Chávez surname was one of the most common in the Middle Valley, the many members of the clan all being descendants of pioneer settler Don Fernando Durán y Chávez. Mariano and José, already among the social elite owing to their prestigious name, both enhanced their standing further by marrying into powerful and wealthy families. Mariano wed a sister of José Leandro Perea of Bernalillo, who was on his way to becoming one of the leading sheep barons of New Mexico. Antonio José married Barbara Armijo of Los Ranchos de Albuquerque, the Armijos, as our narrative will show, being among the most energetic and opportunistic citizens of nineteenth-century Albuquerque.

The two Chávez brothers owned large properties at Los Padillas just below the villa and were already prosperous in ranching before they entered the Santa Fe trade. As their mercantile interests expanded in the 1830s and early 1840s, Antonio José assumed charge of the Missouri end of the business, traveling yearly to Westport and St. Louis to purchase manufactured articles. Mariano, for his part, superintended the export of these goods, plus flocks of sheep, from New Mexico south to Chihuahua and other cities. In 1844, for which we have specific information, Mariano conducted $26,474 worth of merchandise and six thousand sheep valued at $3,000 down to the Chihuahuan markets. These figures, and similar ones for other local merchants, indicate that New Mexico at last was beginning to enjoy a long overdue prosperity.

The new wealth meant that at least upper-class families in the Middle Valley could acquire some of the frills and luxuries that had been in such short supply while Spain ruled. When people like the Chávezes, Armijos, Pereas, Oteros, and Bacas hitched up their wagons and journeyed east to buy trade wares, they usually tacked onto their shopping lists knick-knacks for their own homes and fine gifts for the wife and children. A visitor in 1846 to the Hacienda de Padillas, owned by Mariano Chávez, described its elegant furnishings, most of which had been freighted in over the Santa Fe Trail. "The house is very large . . . with handsome Brussels carpet, crimson worsted curtains, with gilded rings and cornice, white marble slab pier tables—hair and crimson worsted chairs, and candelabra. Since all the Mexicans have the greatest passion for framed pictures and looking glasses, in one room of Chávez's house are eight or ten gilt-framed mirrors all around the wall. All is exceedingly neat and clean." The aristocracy of Albuquerque, materially speaking, had finally come into its own.

The upper crust of the Rio Abajo formed a powerful

clique that easily dominated political, economic, and social life between Bernalillo and Belen. Within this tight circle of families—linked in innumerable lines through constant intermarriage—none was more ambitious or shrewd than the Armijo clan. For the better part of the nineteenth century, the personal fortunes of the Armijos were closely interwoven with the history of Albuquerque.

Founder of the family in New Mexico was José de Armijo, one of the citizens of Zacatecas recruited by Vargas in 1695 to help resettle the Rio Grande Valley. His grandson, Vicente Ferrer Armijo, according to the 1790 census, was a respected rancher living at the Plaza de San Antonio, on the northern outskirts of Albuquerque. Vicente and his wife, Barbara Chávez, had eight children. Four of their sons, Francisco, Ambrosio, Juan, and Manuel, served brief terms as alcalde, or magistrate, of Albuquerque during the 1820s and 1830s. They also held officers' rank in the militia. In 1819 Francisco, for example, commanded the town's Second Squadron. In addition, Ambrosio, Juan, and Manuel were heavily involved in the Santa Fe trade.

By means of family connections, influence in the militia, and his own political acumen, the youngest of the brothers, Manuel Armijo, thrice jockeyed his way into the governor's chair, and, by the sheer weight of personality and cleverness, became the dominant figure in New Mexico during the Mexican period. His true character is difficult to assess because most of those who wrote about him were Americans who, for a variety of reasons, held him in low esteem. One of the most unflattering indictments of his conduct was penned by George Wilkins Kendall, a reporter for the *New Orleans Picayune*. Kendall in 1844 described the governor as a pompous despot, guilty of "assassinations, robberies, violent debauchery, extortions, and innumerable acts of broken faith." He also pictured him as an errant coward whose personal motto accurately reflected the governor's want of courage: *Vale más estar tomado por valiente que serlo.* "It is better to be thought brave than to really be so."

On the credit side, Manuel Armijo unquestionably possessed a strong instinct for survival. Setbacks dogged his career, but repeatedly he managed to recover and turn ill fortune to his own advantage. Amid the storms and quicksands of New Mexican politics, that was no mean feat. At best, then, it can be said that he was a man of energy, but of few scruples. Some would have added that he was a clever politician, but one with all the personal charm of a snapping turtle.

Armijo's first term as governor, 1827 to 1829, ended under a cloud. He resigned in the latter year apparently to avoid a federal investigation of irregularities into the conduct of his office. At that point, he retired to his home in Albuquerque to become alcalde, but having tasted the power that went with the governorship, he kept casting wistful glances toward Santa Fe.

An opportunity to reenter the political arena finally came in 1837. A new governor, brash and young Albino Pérez, from Mexico City had been ordered by the national government to impose direct taxes and at the same time reform the New Mexican's lackadaisical ways of administering provincial affairs. These measures, regarded as outside interference, sparked deep resentment on the Upper Rio Grande and fueled a plot among certain sectors of the populace to overthrow Pérez. Since conspiracies are conceived in secrecy, names of the participants, their plans, and motives are often lost to history. Nevertheless, circumstantial evidence strongly points to Manuel Armijo as one of the ringleaders. He was hoping, it seems, to step in and claim Albino Pérez's place, should the governor be ousted. But in the sequence of bloody events that followed, matters took an altogether unexpected turn.

Open insurrection broke forth in August 1837 among farming folk and Pueblo Indians north of Santa Fe. Governor Pérez mustered a small force of reluctant followers and confidently marched out to disperse the rebels. In a skirmish near San Ildefonso, his men were defeated and he was obliged to race for the capital with a frenzied mob at his heels. Shortly thereafter, the governor was captured and decapitated while members of his staff were tortured and killed.

News of these barbarous doings upriver threw the rich dons of the Rio Abajo into a panic. As much as they may have disliked Albino Pérez, they were in no mood to support a rabble movement that defied established authority. Catching the drift of sentiment among his neighbors, Manuel Armijo perceived at once where his own interests lay. He now announced his opposition to the uprising and invited others to join him in putting it down. At a meeting held September 8 at Tomé, just below Albuquerque, the elite of the Middle Valley convened and issued a manifesto calling for vigorous suppression of the forces of anarchy that had seized control of Santa Fe. Armijo was the first to affix his signature and rubric to the document.

Mariano Chávez, also in attendance, addressed the gathering and made a dramatic nomination. "I know of no one better qualified to lead our army than Manuel Armijo," he declared in stentorian tones. "Therefore, I ask this assemblage to declare him to be our leader." And without a dissenting vote, that was done.

With the entire militia of the Rio Abajo at his back, Armijo grandly marched away and within a few days occupied the capital, which the rebels had vacated upon his approach. Promptly he dispatched couriers to Mexico City with an exaggerated account of his exploits. He portrayed himself as the savior of New Mexico, a claim that soon won him confirmation as governor and supreme commander of military forces. With his hand thus strengthened, Armijo the following January led his soldiers north to the Santa Cruz Valley where the insurgents had again collected, scattered them in a fierce battle, and summarily executed the captured leaders.

Over the next several years, Manuel Armijo, who now sported the title of general as well as governor, consolidated his political power, stepped up his commercial activities in the Santa Fe trade, and acquired significant new land holdings. When in 1841 an expedition of 320 men from the newly independent Republic of Texas invaded eastern New Mexico, he took the field with his troops and soon had the entire party under wraps. Newsman George Wilkins Kendall was one of the prisoners, and it was largely because of the abuse he and his companions suffered at the governor's hands that he later wrote about Armijo in such uncomplimentary terms.

Marched south under heavy guard toward Mexico where a jail awaited them, the Texan captives passed through Albuquerque. There, as Kendall later informed his readers, Governor Armijo maintained a hacienda, a fine estate he had purchased with the proceeds of his cheating, stealing, and gambling transactions. The governor resided at home only part of the time—for the rest, being occupied with his duties in Santa Fe—but his family remained at Albuquerque year-round. Armijo's wife, Trinidad Gabaldón, he described as a "gross, brazen-faced woman . . . contaminated with every depraved habit to human nature." Evidently, the newsman's hatred for the governor spilled over to include the governor's wife. Other Americans subsequently spoke of Señora Armijo in gentle and charitable terms.

To other ladies he met, Kendall responded more favorably. Albuquerque, he averred, was famed for the beauty of its women. "It was there that I saw a perfect specimen of female loveliness. The girl was poor, yet there was an air of grace, a charm about her, that neither birth nor fortune can bestow. She was standing upon a mud wall, the taper fingers of her right hand supporting a large pumpkin upon her head, while her left was gracefully resting upon her hip. Her figure was faultless and even the chisel of Praxiteles himself never modeled ankles of such pure and classic elegance. . . . Among the crowds of beauty her image will stand out in bold relief, and not one of those who saw her on the day we passed through Albuquerque will ever forget her."

While the Armijos, Chávezes, and other patrician families of the valley devoted themselves to politics, military affairs, and commercial enterprises, Albuquerque's peasant folk—which included Kendall's pretty pumpkin girl—carried on the even tempo of their simple lives, much as they always had. Times were changing, but as yet at such a slow pace that the average man was scarcely aware of it.

Free public schools, for example, something that had been

lacking under Spain, had been introduced by the government of the Mexican Republic. But in Albuquerque, as elsewhere in New Mexico, these were never more than feeble and ineffectual institutions, completely incapable of banishing the illiteracy that almost universally prevailed. The town's alcalde and municipal council exercised administrative responsibility over the school, teacher, and pupils, but they were dependent for operating funds upon appropriations by the legislative assembly in Santa Fe. Such funds, for the teacher's salary and school supplies, came irregularly, when at all, and in paltry sums.

Ambrosio Armijo, alcalde of Albuquerque in 1828, in desperation wrote the governor, his brother Manuel, asking him to pull strings on behalf of the local school because it possessed no paper or books. If the governor could not procure both of these necessary items, then Ambrosio declared he would settle for "one or the other." Three years later, it is recorded that the provincial assembly allocated the magnificent sum of 40 pesos so that Albuquerque's teacher, Antonio Ruíz, might purchase a year's worth of supplies for his pupils. The niggardly support of education seems to have caused no great outcry among the public, mainly because of a general apathy toward the entire issue. Alcaldes, who doubled as truant officers, found that parents were uncooperative—children were needed at home and time spent in school was time lost from work. The gentry, unlike the common folk, placed a high value on education, but aware of the deficiencies of the local system, they sent their sons east to St. Louis or south to Durango to be enrolled in tuition-supported church and private schools.

Conditions of the churches in the Middle Valley very nearly

matched those of the schools. Among the Franciscans, the missionary zeal that had animated the order during the colonial years practically vanished during the Mexican period. As the older friars died, none were sent to replace them. Those few who remained were forced to ride an ever wider circuit, spreading their labors thin. When in 1833 Bishop José Antonio Laureano de Zubiría journeyed up from Durango to make an episcopal visit, he found spiritual life among the New Mexicans in a sad and neglected state. At each community he inspected the furnishings and property of the church and conducted the sacrament of Confirmation (at Albuquerque this occurred on August 9), but nothing he saw gave much room for hope. Religious services were imperfectly and irregularly performed, attendance was down, and attention to the needs of the Indians was in serious decline.

The bishop took special exception to the Brotherhood of Penitentes, an order of laymen that engaged in bloody acts of penitence and held mock crucifixions on Good Friday. Most of the Penitentes resided in remote villages of the north, but some were scattered through the Middle Valley, with a heavy concentration around the village of Tomé. In a stern pastoral letter, Zubiría denounced the Brotherhood, terming it illegal and calling for its suppression. In the same document, he exhorted the people to pay closer heed to their religious duties.

By 1846, New Mexicans were in dire need of whatever comfort their religion could afford. Even greater was a need for wise and inspired leadership to help them confront a crisis developing in the East, one that carried the potential punch of a cyclone. United States–Mexican relations had deteriorated steadily after American settlers in Mexico's province of Texas declared independence in 1836. Refusing to acknowledge loss of the territory, Mexico made several unsuccessful attempts to recover it, prior to the United States annexation of Texas late in 1845. When the Mexican government sent troops across the lower Rio Grande to defend its claim in the spring of 1846, a fight with American troops ensued. A few weeks later, on May 11, President James K. Polk went before Congress and read a formal declaration of war. From that moment forward, the fate of New Mexico and other territories on Mexico's northern frontier was sealed, though some months elapsed before citizens there were made aware of that fact.

Albuquerque's Manuel Armijo, in the midst of his third term as governor, appeared to be New Mexico's man of the hour when war broke forth. With his customary bluster, he issued high-sounding patriotic appeals to the populace, warning them to be ready, at the first sign of an American invasion, to answer a call to arms. In consultation with his lieutenants, the governor laid plans to fortify the mountain pass at the mouth of Apache Canyon, fifteen miles east of the capital. That strategic site, commanding access to the final leg of the Santa Fe Trail, seemed the best place to try to hold back an invading army.

And an army, indeed, was on its way—from Fort Leavenworth, Kansas. Under the command of General Stephen Watts Kearny, the force was composed of regular infantry, dragoon, and artillery companies, plus a large contingent of hard-fighting Missouri volunteers. These men knew of Manual Armijo by reputation—of his mistreatment of Texas prisoners in 1841, and of his high-handed dealings with some of the Santa Fe traders. So as they marched west to the conquest of New

Mexico, there was a spring in their gait, put there by the expectation that they would soon have the chance to call Manuel Armijo to account.

Perhaps fearful of just such an eventuality, the governor took elaborate pains to ensure that nothing like that would happen. Upon learning that Kearny's troops had occupied Las Vegas on New Mexico's easternmost fringe of settlement and were en route to the capital, Manuel Armijo ordered the trumpets sounded. At the front of a rag-tag army composed of regulars, militiamen, and a scattering of Pueblo Indians, he rode out to Apache Canyon, where he had a few breastworks built. Before the construction proceeded very far, the governor called a halt and announced that he was withdrawing and giving up the game. Several of his officers, made of sterner stuff, threatened to shoot him if he did not stand and fight. Armijo paid no attention, and instead calmly climbed into his American-built carriage and drove south to the village of Galisteo, headed for Mexico. In his haste to be gone, it seems the governor neglected making a side trip to Albuquerque, to bid his wife Trinidad good-bye. Rather, he directed his flight down the east slope of the Sandia and Manzano mountains, crossing into the Rio Grande Valley at Abó Pass. He must have gotten some message home, however, for he was soon joined on the road by a wagon train bearing personal possessions and a goodly stock of merchandise brought earlier over the Santa Fe Trail. If he must retreat into exile, Manuel Armijo had no intention of going as a pauper. Señora Armijo was not with the wagons. She had been left in Albuquerque.

Far down in the desert wastes of Chihuahua, a young British adventurer, George Ruxton, heading toward New

Mexico, encountered the fleeing official. "The runaway governor of New Mexico, General Armijo," he informs us, "was traveling in company with his caravan on his way to Mexico City, to give an account of shameful cowardice in surrendering Santa Fe to the Americans without a show of resistance. I stopped and had a long chat with Armijo, who . . . rolled out of his American dearborn, and inquired the price of cotton goods in Durango, he having seven wagonloads with him." The former governor, it would appear, was more interested for the moment in business than in politics.

The failure to show resistance, of which Ruxton spoke, had allowed the army of General Kearny to march unopposed into the streets of Santa Fe and hoist the American flag over the plaza. But Armijo's flight had also deprived the Missouri boys of their opportunity to settle accounts. A few days after the fall of the capital, however, a rumor circulated that suggested there might yet be a chance to meet the governor in battle.

General Kearny received word that Manuel Armijo had returned with troops from Chihuahua and was in the vicinity of Albuquerque, rallying the Abajeños (as people of the Rio Abajo were called) with a view to recovering Santa Fe from the Americans. Although the report was entirely without foundation, Kearny thought it wise to lead part of his troops downriver for a personal look at the situation. As he emerged with his cavalcade of seven hundred men from The Narrows at the upper end of the Middle Valley, the general was greeted by a throng of people, representing not an opposing army, but a horde of venders eager to sell their baskets of grapes, melons, and eggs. The soldiers, who had been on short rations for days, grabbed the opportunity to swap a straight pin for a bunch of grapes, or a button off their blouse for a melon.

As the Americans marched toward Albuquerque, the crowd of sellers and curiosity-seekers swelled into the hundreds. The whole affair had the air of a Fourth of July frolic. Nowhere was there the slightest sign of hostility. "The people received us kindly," remarked one young soldier. "They seem to be well pleased with the change of government & the idea of being considered as citizens of the American Republic. They say that Armijo has gone to the Devil."

At Bernalillo, Kearny and his officers were entertained in the largest house of the district, the residence of the lordly Perea family. Most of the adult members had been over the Santa Fe Trail to Missouri on more than one occasion, and several younger sons, fluent in English, had attended Catholic schools in St. Louis and New York City. While servant girls pattered about, the American officers accepted plates and spoons of solid New Mexican silver, "clumsily worked in the country," and helped themselves to a table loaded with grapes, sponge-cake, and local wine. Lieutenant W. H. Emory, mingling with the others, took reproving note of the *sala*, or large reception hall. "The walls are hung with miserable pictures of the saints, crosses innumerable, and Yankee mirrors without number. These last are suspended entirely out of reach; and if one wishes to shave or adjust his toilet, he must do so without the aid of the mirror, be there ever so many in the chamber."

It was early September as the men approached Albuquerque. The corn was being taken in, the yield of the vineyards borne to the wine presses, and droves of mules driven to the open threshing floors where their flinty hooves would separate the newly harvested wheat from its chaff. The valley swarmed with waterfowl—ducks, wild geese, sandhill cranes, blue heron, and even a few pelicans—but for the most part they remained undisturbed except, as Emory comments, "when some American levels his rifle." The curious adobe fences bordering the road, their tops planted with cactus to keep trespassers out of the fields, drew the attention of the marchers, as did the elaborate network of irrigation ditches that appeared strange to men raised in a land of abundant rainfall.

Among the half dozen or so of Kearney's followers who were keeping a daily journal, most mentioned the high density of farms in the Middle Valley. As one diarist phrased it: "On both banks of the river, the towns, villages, and ranchos or farm houses cluster so thickly together that it presents the appearance of one continued village from Algodones to San Tomé, a distance of nearly sixty miles." Albuquerque itself, the writer related, stretched some seven or eight miles up and down the river. To get to the plaza, another soldier complained, "I rode for miles as through a straggling village." Evidently the helter-skelter layout of the old villa, referred to by eighteenth-century writers, still prevailed.

When the general and his command paraded into the center of Albuquerque, they received an unexpectedly cordial welcome—one, in fact, that bordered on the tumultuous. The long lines of men followed by the artillery and baggage train formed ranks in front of the church. Brown faces pressing close on all sides seemed duly impressed by the American banner and the company colors, which streamed and snapped in the fall breeze. There was much cheering and noise and at one point, in the best tradition of a Hollywood musical script, "a song of welcome by the inhabitants." At least that is how a youthful trooper remembered it years afterward. Adding to the uproar, members of the Albuquerque militia, positioned on the flat roof of the church, fired a twenty-gun-salute, using old Spanish *escopetas,* or muskets. With these demonstrations of friendship, Kearny rose before the assembled populace and administered the oath of allegiance to the United States government. Henceforth, for good or ill, Albuquerqueans were American citizens.

We can but wonder what the town's first lady, Doña Trinidad Armijo, thought of these ceremonies, which witnessed the transfer of the province, formerly ruled by her husband, into the hands of foreigners. Upon meeting the lady a few months before Kearny's arrival in Albuquerque, Alfred Waugh, a traveling Irish artist, described her as an intelligent woman who deported herself with much propriety. Later, the Britisher Ruxton caught a glimpse of her seated in the window of her home: "I had a good view of the lady who was once celebrated as the belle of New Mexico. She is now a fat, comely dame of forty, with the remains of considerable beauty, but quite *passée.*" Bereft of her husband and of her social position because of his hasty flight, Señora Armijo appears, nevertheless, to have preserved her equanimity and pride. And she possessed also the large town house, referred to in some accounts as an adobe mansion, similar in style to the Governors Palace in Santa Fe, with a *portal* entirely across the front and ornamental tinned doors.

Others of Manuel Armijo's Albuquerque relatives evidently suffered not the slightest disturbance in their households or business affairs as the town passed into American hands. In truth, like most of New Mexico's privileged dons, they were well situated to take advantage of the new order. For them, the political change meant more profits. A conspicuous example was offered by one of Manuel's nephews, whose store on the plaza Susan Magoffin, wife of a merchant, visited late in 1846.

"At Albuquerque," she jotted in her diary, "we stopped for a few moments at the store of Don Rafael Armijo, which notwithstanding the Sabbath was opened. While they were counting some money my husband was receiving, I stepped in to take a look at the premises. The building was very spacious, with wide portals in front. Inside is the patio, the store occupying a long room on the street. This is filled with all kinds of little fixings, dry goods, groceries, hardware &c."

Leaving the town on Saturday, Kearny and his column proceeded south to the village of Tomé to complete their survey of the Middle Valley. By chance, a religious fiesta was in progress so that the men from Missouri received an introduction to merrymaking, New Mexican style. All roads leading into Tomé were crowded with people, some walking, others riding in ox carts, in carriages, or on horseback or burro. At nightfall the entire place burst into flame as a myriad of skyrockets, trailing zigzag streams of sparks, soared hundreds of feet into the air, and small bonfires of pine knots were lighted on every housetop and on the roof of the church. A discharge of musketry and a clattering of the mission bell, creating a thunderous din for four continuous hours, were meant to contribute to the festive atmosphere, although to the awe-struck Americans the decibel of noise seemed more likely to render the throng of fun-seekers totally deaf. Fifteen hundred persons, according to one estimate, squeezed into the public square, took seats on the bare, hard-packed sod, and watched entranced as a Spanish folk comedy was performed by a group of actors on an improvised stage. At the same time, the side streets were filled with people dancing, gambling, horseracing, or selling baskets of baked goods and fruit. The pandemonium persisted without let-up far into the evening.

At sunup, the fiesta was renewed with appropriate religious observances. The church, packed to overflowing, was lighted by twenty-four candles. General Kearny and his staff officers, who thought it politic to attend, were handed tapers. As one of the enlisted men observed with a snicker, "They looked and no doubt felt supremely ridiculous, each one holding a long, greasy tallow candle in his hand, which was to be blown out and relighted at certain intervals during the ceremony." Throughout the service, loud singing, instrumental music, and the firing of musketry shook the rafters, so that the voice of the priest on the altar was scarcely heard. "Was this serving God in spirit and in truth," asked one of the soldiers rhetorically.

The local congregation must have thought so, for when the ritual inside was done, they moved outdoors where there was nothing to confine their pious enthusiasm. The padre led the way, accompanied by four men who held a gilded canopy over his head and used their elbows to nudge a path through the crowd. In the train went also lads with muskets, who kept up a steady firing into the air, and altar boys, throwing skyrockets aloft. "With their continual racket," said Private John T. Hughes, "they made the heavens dizzy with streams of fire."

Next day, General Kearny, much relived to be done with the business of fiestas, and having ascertained that no sentiment for resistance existed in the Rio Abajo, faced his men about and pointed them toward Santa Fe. The first night on the back trail they spent at Albuquerque, where many of the troops were lodged in the extensive barracks adjacent to Manuel Armijo's home. Young Ruxton advises us that the former governor had constructed these quarters to accommodate the large military escort that always attended him on frequent trips down from Santa Fe. The barracks must have been frugally built and with little thought for comfort, as was the prevailing custom in New Mexico. Said one of the Americans who found shelter there: "In order to show the limited size of our quarters, the room that I and eight others were in was only fourteen feet by eight. Here we cooked, ate, and slept; and had, as it may well be presumed, close stowage at night. It was lighted by a window hole about fifteen inches square."

Rough as these lodgings were, they were destined to see more service, for within a few weeks a detachment of the First Dragoons was posted at Albuquerque under the command of Captain J. H. Burgwin, for the purpose of protecting the surrounding countryside from the Navajos. One of the things Kearny had promised, upon taking custody of New Mexico, was to put a stop to hostile Indian raids. But that was a gift far beyond his capacity to deliver, as he was soon made aware. Through the early weeks of September 1846, reports of Navajo forays in the Middle Valley reached his ears almost daily. In the environs of Albuquerque, twelve thousand sheep were stolen on a single day, and while that was considered something of a record by local ranchers, the news was greeted with no great astonishment, so common had large-scale thefts become. In frustration the general endorsed guerrilla warfare against the Indian miscreants. His proclamation on the subject read, in part:

In consequence of the frequent and almost daily outrages committed by the Navajo upon the Persons & Property of the Inhabitants of the Rio Abajo, . . . now be it known that I, Brigadier General S. W. Kearny, hereby authorize all the Mexicans and Pueblos living in the said . . . Rio Abajo, to form War Parties, to march into the Country of their enemies, the Navajos, to recover their property, to make reprisals and obtain redress for the many insults received from them.

Kearny departed for the conquest of California on September 25 after erecting the scaffolding of a civil government in New Mexico. He left the territory under the care of Colonel Alexander Doniphan, who had instructions to take some of the American garrison and invade Navajoland. His goal was to arrange a peace treaty if possible, and if not, then to wage war. On a snowy November 21, Doniphan met with some five hundred members of the tribe at Ojo del Oso (Bear Spring), a noted landmark 150 miles west of Albuquerque, and concluded a treaty. Unfortunately, it held up for less than a year, because while the Navajos were perfectly willing to regard the Americans as friends, they could not bring themselves to make peace with their hereditary enemies, the New Mexicans. So the raids on Albuquerque and other valley towns continued, and their peoples soon grew accustomed to patrols of blue-jacketed soldiers dashing back and forth over the dusty roads girding the Rio Grande.

In the short space of a quarter century, Albuquerqueans had seen their land shuffled from the rule of Spain to that of Mexico, and finally to the United States. These political changes, fundamental though they may have been, were quickly overshadowed by far greater social, economic, and cultural changes. The growth of the Santa Fe trade and Kearny's conquest of 1846 marked the beginnings of the Americanization of Albuquerque. That process, developing slowly at first, would not come full circle to completion until 1949 when the Old Town, centering on the plaza of colonial days, would finally be annexed and absorbed by the New Town, the twentieth-century metropolis that sprang from the railroad boom of the 1880s.

# Suggested Readings

Adams, Eleanor B., and Fray Angelico Chávez, eds. and trans. *The Missions of New Mexico: 1776*. Albuquerque: University of New Mexico Press, 1956.

Archibald, Robert. "Cañon de Carnué: Settlement of a Grant." In *New Mexico Historical Review* [NMHR] 51 (1976): 313–28.

Armijo, Isidro, trans. "Noticias of Juan Candelaria." In *NMHR* 4 (1929): 274–97.

Bloom, Lansing B. "Albuquerque and Galisteo, Certificate of their Founding: 1706." In *NMHR* 10 (1935): 48–50.

Bolton, Herbert E. *Coronado: Knight of Pueblos and Plains*. Albuquerque: University of New Mexico Press, 1949.

Chávez, Fray Angelico. "The Albuquerque Story." In *New Mexico Magazine* 34 (January 1956): 18–19, 50–51.

———. *From the Beginning: A Historical Survey of San Felipe Neri Church*. Albuquerque: privately printed, 1972.

Cooke, Philip St. George. *The Conquest of New Mexico and California*. New York: G. P. Putnam's Sons, 1878.

Edwards, Frank S. *A Campaign in New Mexico*. Repr. ed.; Albuquerque: University of New Mexico Press, 1996.

Fergusson, Erna. *Albuquerque.* Albuquerque: Merle Armitage Editions, 1947.

Flint, Richard. *Great Cruelties Have Been Reported: The 1544 Investigation of the Coronado Expedition.* Dallas: Southern Methodist University Press, 2002.

Gallagher, Peter. "The Founding of Albuquerque." In *Rio Grande History* 7 (1977): 2–5.

Greenleaf, Richard E. "Atrisco and Las Ciruelas: 1722–1769." In *NMHR* 42 (1967): 5–25.

———. "The Founding of Albuquerque: 1706." In *NMHR* 39 (1964): 1–15.

Hendricks, Rick, ed. "The Last Years of Francisco Cuervo y Valdés." In *La Crónica de Nuevo México* (Historical Society of New Mexico) 36 (July 1993): 2–3.

Kessell, John L. *Spain in the Southwest.* Norman: University of Oklahoma Press, 2002.

———, with Rick Hendricks, et al. *The Journals of don Diego de Vargas: New Mexico, 1691–1704.* 6 vols. Albuquerque: University of New Mexico Press, 1989–2002.

Lecompte, Janet. "Manuel Armijo's Family History." In *NMHR* 48 (1973): 251–58.

Metzgar, Joseph V. "The Atrisco Land Grant: 1692–1977." In *NMHR* 52 (1977): 269–96.

Moorhead, Max L. *New Mexico's Royal Road: Trade and Travel on the Chihuahua Trail.* Repr. ed.; Norman: University of Oklahoma Press, 1995.

Pearce, Thomas M. *The Dukes of Albuquerque—Albuquerque, New Mexico—Old Spain and New Spain.* Albuquerque: Albuquerque Historical Society, 1977.

Rios-Bustamante, Antonio José. "New Mexico in the Eighteenth Century." In *Aztlán* 7 (1978): 357–90.

Simmons, Marc. *Spanish Government in New Mexico.* Repr. ed.; Albuquerque: University of New Mexico Press, 1990.

Sinclair, John. "The Place Where DeVargas Died." In *New Mexico Magazine* 54 (August 1976): 33–38, 43–45.

Stanley, F. *The Duke City: The Story of Albuquerque, New Mexico: 1706–1956*. Pampa, Tex.: privately printed, 1963.

Steele, Thomas J., S.J. *Works and Days: A History of San Felipe Neri Church*. Albuquerque: Albuquerque Museum, 1983.

Weber, David J. *The Spanish Frontier in North America*. New Haven, Conn.: Yale University Press, 1992.

# Index

acequias, 73
Acoma Pueblo, 55
agriculture: in 1840s, 148; available land, 13–14; farmers, 104; flooding, 73; settlement pattern, 65
Alameda Pueblo: and Coronado, 5; first visitas, 13; and the Pueblo Revolt, 23; rebuilding of, 56, 84–85; uprising, 20
Alameda village, 91, 130
Albuquerque: during 1600s, 18; 1789 census, 110–12; 1790 census, 105; 1822 census, 130–31; and American trade, 135; and the Apaches, 82; charter families, 58, 59, 60; and the Comanches, 82; founding site, 17; during the Mexican period, 133–34;

military protection, 48, 52, 57, 76, 78–79; militia, 79, 110; naming of, 66–69, x; plaza, 61, 64, 130; population growth, 105, 109–12, 130–31; and the railroad, 49–51; settlement pattern, 63–64, 65; as a villa, 49–50, 64; and water rights, 51
Alburquerque, Duke of: as Albuquerque's namesake, x; and Cuervo, 68–69; history of, 65–66; signature, 38
Alburquerque, Spain, 39, 65
alcalde mayors: of Albuquerque, 58; Dúran y Chávez, 28; García de Noriega, 17; in the Middle Valley, 14; Treból Navarro, 97–99
Alcanfor, 4–5, 7
alliance fund, 131–32

Alvarado, Hernando de, 2, 4, 7
Anaya, Cristóbal, 15–16, 22
Anza, Juan Bautista de, 83
Apaches: at Albuquerque, 82; and
    the alliance fund, 131–32; at
    Carnué, 95; Faraon band, 78;
    and the Pueblo Indians, 19; in
    the Sandias, 78; and trade,
    75–76
Arenal Pueblo, 5, 6
Armijo, Ambrosio, 142
Armijo, Barbara, 135
Armijo, Don Rafael, 150
Armijo family, 134, 135, 137
Armijo, José de, 137
Armijo, Manuel, 43; according to
    Kendall, 137–38; in
    Albuquerque, 140–41; military
    barracks, 152; and Pérez,
    138–40; retreat to Chihuahua,
    145–46; and Texans, 140–41;
    war with U.S., 144
Armijo, Trinidad (Gabaldón), 141,
    149
Armijo, Vincente Ferrer, 137
Arteaga, Manuel de, 113
Atrisco village, 57, 93–94, 105
ayuntamientos, 128–29, 130

Baca, Bartolomé, 133
Baca estancia, 15
Baca, Josepha, 106
Baca, Joseph Antonio, 95
Baca, Manuel, 54
Barela de Losada, Pedro, 19
Benavides, Alonso de, 12–13
Bernalillo: early status, 30–31;
    founding of, 28; its namesake,
    15; militia, 54

Bosque Grande de Doña Luisa, 18
Burgwin, J. H., 152
Bustamante Tagle, Bernardo de, 88

Cabezon Peak, 32
Camino Real: and American trade,
    135; Hacienda de Mejía, 18, 25;
    and merchant convoys, 108–9;
    and the Middle Valley, 12;
    Spanish caravans, 41
Candelaria, Juan, 59
Cañon de Carnué, 48, 94–95
Carlos, Juan, 12
Carnué village, 95–99
Carvajal estancia, 15
Catholicism, 2. See also churches;
    priests
Cebolleta, 133
Cebolleta Mountains, 32
cemeteries, 115, 120
Chacón, Don Joseph. See Peñuela,
    Marqués de la
Chávez, Antonio José, 135, 136
Chávez, Barbara, 137
Chávez, Don Nicolás, 100–104
Chávez, Fernando, 54
Chávez, Francisco Javier, 135
Chávez, Mariano, 135, 136,
    139–40
churches: apathy, 116; first in
    Albuquerque, 115–16;
    Franciscans, 117–21; Indian
    rights, 2; during the Mexican
    period, 142–43; San Felipe de
    Neri, 117; secular priests,
    118–21
Cochiti Pueblo, 55

Marín del Valle, Francisco, 79
Martínez, Félix, 76–77
Mejía, Hacienda de, 18, 25
Melgares, Facundo, 132
men, 111–12, 116
Mendinueta, Pedro Fermín de,
    96–98
Mendoza, Viceroy Don Antonio, 3
Mesa Prieta, 32
Mexico: Independence, 129–30;
    and New Mexico, 131; soldiers,
    44; war with U.S., 143–44
Middle Valley, 12, 14, 55–57
military: at Acoma Pueblo, 55; and
    the militia, 54; protection, 48,
    52, 57, 76, 78–79
militia: Albuquerque, 79, 110;
    Bernalillo, 54; and merchant
    convoys, 109; during the
    Mexican period, 133–34
mining, 29
missions, 12, 20–21
Moho Pueblo, 6
Montaño, Antonio, 98
Montaño, Bernabé, 92–93
Montes Vigil, Francisco, 85
Montoya, Diego de, 54, 90
municipalities, 29

Napoleonic Wars, 127–28
The Narrows of the Rio Grande,
    14
Navajos: at Jemez Pueblo, 77–78;
    during the Mexican period,
    132–33, 134; in the Puerco
    Valley, 94; at Santa Clara
    Pueblo, 78; and the U.S.
    military, 152–53

Ojo del Oso, 153
Olivares, Francisco, 120
Oñate, Juan de, 10–11
Ortiz Mountain, 33
Otermín, Antonio de, 22, 22–25

Páez Hurtado, Juan, 27, 51
Pajarito, 106, 130
paraje, 18
partidario, 105
Peña, Juan de la, 85–86
Peñalosa, Diego de, 19, 56
Penitentes, 143
Peñuela, Marqués de la, 69, 77, 85,
    90
Peralta, Don Pedro de, 12
Perea estancia, 15
Perea, José Leandro, 135
Pérez, Albino, 138–39
Pike, Zebulon Montgomery: in
    Albuquerque, 120, 125–26;
    his capture, 124; in Chihuahua,
    126; on New Mexico's econo-
    my, 127
Pino, Pedro Bautista, 128
Pino, Pedro Ignacio, 87–88
Pojoaque Pueblo, 59, 62
population growth, 105, 109–12,
    130–31
priests: first in New Mexico, 8–9;
    Franciscans, 117–18, 119–21;
    during the Mexican period, 143;
    secular, 118–21
Puaray Pueblo, 9, 10, 13
Pueblo Revolt, 20–22
puestos, 29

Quivira, 7

trade. *See also* economy; American, 134–35; and the Apaches, 75–76; currency, 106–7; and merchant convoys, 108–9; and merchant wealth, 136; during Mexican-American war, 146–47; regulations, 122–23; and wool, 107–8

Treból Navarro, Don Francisco, 97–99

Trujillo, Doña Luisa, 17–18

Trujillo, Francisco, 17, 67

Ulibarrí, Juan de, 47

United States, 123–24, 134–35, 143–44

Utes, 131–32

vaccines, 113

Valencia village, 82, 87

Vallas Caldera, 33

Varela de Losada, Pedro, 19

Vargas Zapata y Luján, Don Diego de: application of the Recopilacíon, 58; his death, 30; at Mejía, 25; and Santa Fe, 26, 27

Vélez Cachupín, Tomás, 79, 93

villas: charter ceremony, 59–60; defined, 29; regulations for chartering, 47; settlement pattern, 64

visitas, 13

Vizcarra, José Antonio, 134

weather conditions, 4–5, 21, 52–53, 100

weaving industry, 109

women, 111–12, 116

wool trade, 107–8

Zabaleta, Juan de, 84

Zia Pueblo, 35

Zuñi Pueblo, 52, 55